BY CLAYTON ESHLEMAN:

Mexico & North (1962)
Residence on Earth (translations of Pablo Neruda) (1962)
The Chavin Illumination (1965)
State of the Union (translations of Aimé Césaire, with Denis Kelly) (1966)
Lachrymae Mateo (1966)
Walks (1967)
Poemas Humanos/Human Poems (translations of César Vallejo) (1968)
Brother Stones (with William Paden's woodcuts) (1968)
Cantaloups & Splendor (1968)
T'ai (1969)
The House of Okumura (1969)
The House of Ibuki (1969)
Indiana (1969)
Yellow River Record (1969)
A Pitchblende (1969)
Bearings (1971)
Altars (1971)
A Caterpillar Anthology (editor & contributor) (1971)
The Sanjo Bridge (1972)
Coils (1973)
Human Wedding (1973)
Aux Morts (1974)
Spain, Take this Cup from Me (translations of Vallejo, with José Rubia Barcia) (1974)
Letter to André Breton (translation of Antonin Artaud) (1974)
Realignment (with drawings by Nora Jaffe) (1974)
Portrait of Francis Bacon (1975)
To Have Done with the Judgment of God (translation of Artaud, with Norman Glass) (1975)
The Gull Wall (1975)
Cogollo (1976)
Artaud the Mômo (translation of Artaud, with Norman Glass) (1976)
The Woman Who Saw through Paradise (1976)
Grotesca (1977)
On Mules Sent from Chavin (1977)
Core Meander (1977)
The Gospel of Celine Arnauld (1977)
Battles in Spain (translations of Vallejo, with José Rubia Barcia) (1978)
The Name Encanyoned River (1978)
What She Means (1978)
César Vallejo: The Complete Posthumous Poetry (with José Rubia Barcia) (1978)
A Note on Apprenticeship (1979)
The Lich Gate (1980)
Nights We Put the Rock Together (1980)
Our Lady of the Three-Pronged Devil (1980)
Hades in Manganese (1981)
Foetus Graffiti (1981)
Antonin Artaud: Four Texts (with Norman Glass) (1982)
Visions of the Fathers of Lascaux (1983)
Fracture (1983)
Aimé Césaire: The Collected Poetry (with Annette Smith) (1983)
Given Giving (translations of Michel Deguy) (1984)
Chanson (translation of Artaud, with A. James Arnold) (1985)
The Name Encanyoned River: Selected Poems 1960-1985 (1986)

CLAYTON ESHLEMAN

THE NAME ENCANYONED RIVER

SELECTED POEMS 1960-1985

Introduction by Eliot Weinberger

Black Sparrow Press • Santa Barbara • 1986

THE NAME ENCANYONED RIVER: SELECTED POEMS 1960-1985. Copyright © 1962, 1967, 1969, 1971, 1973, 1975, 1978, 1981, 1983, 1986 by Clayton Eshleman.

ACKNOWLEDGEMENTS

The poems in Sections I-III have previously been published in various books. At the end of each poem is the year of composition and the book the poem appeared in. Some of the poems in Section IV have appeared in *Blast 3, Bluefish, Exquisite Corpse, Iron Rations* (London), *Pequod, Scripsi* (Australia), *Sulfur,* and *Temblor.*

I would especially like to acknowledge the following: Gerald Burns, Hayden Carruth, David MacLagan, Donald Wesling, and Alan Williamson, for their suggestions as to what to include in this collection; Paul Christensen, Caryl Eshleman, Leland Hickman, Jed Rasula, and Eliot Weinberger, for not only their suggestions but their help in organizing the structure of the book.

LIBRARY OF CONGRESS CATALOGING IN PUBLICATION DATA

Eshleman, Clayton, 1935-
  The name encanyoned river.

  I. Title.
PS3555.S5N3   1985   811'.54   85-26648

ISBN 0-87685-653-9
ISBN 0-87685-652-0 (pbk.)
ISBN 0-87685-654-7 (signed ed.)

"You cannot
heed the negative, so might go on to undeserved doom
. . . must therefore loose yourself within a pattern's mastery
that you can conceive, that you can yield to — by which
also you win and gain mastery and happiness which is your
own from birth."

— Hart Crane (1931)

CONTENTS

III / THE SEPARATION CONTINUUM

IV / ANTIPHONAL SWING

INTRODUCTION

In a recent survey, 90% of American high school students stated that they do not believe in the existence of the future. What was once a philosophical proposition, an aesthetic obsession, has filtered down to become, for the children of the millennium, a reigning truth. Nothing is certain; the sun may not rise tomorrow.

At the moment of doubt, worlds open up, and each fresh report from those strange worlds leads to further doubt. This has been the century of the invention of the unconscious (personal and collective), of anthropology, paleontology, of science fiction and scientific cosmological speculation: the creation of thousands of other worlds, terrestrial and extraterrestrial, apparent to the eye of a traveler or beyond the reach of the telescope, buried in the earth, hidden within an unsuspecting mind. It has been the century where physical science and mathematics are built on fundamental contradiction, where the increasingly precise observation and description of the natural sciences leads only to essential inexplicability.

At the moment of doubt, possibilities become limitless—all of them equally impossible. For poetry, the end of certainty has meant, first, that the poem can no longer be a discrete object, the "poem itself," for behind every poem there is another poem (written or unwritten) that contradicts it, and behind that, another poem. The poem is a becoming, not a being; and the poem, breaking out of its isolation, can no longer be contained by the traditional forms. There is no closure: the poem is only a passage leading to another.

Second, it has meant that the poem must be open to everything, and moreover, that everything must come into the poem. Most of the best American poets of the century have demanded the admission of that which was previously excluded: history, economics, found objects, colloquial speech, the works of the Machine Age, the unbeautiful, scientific vocabulary, frank autobiography, the whole body, non-human species, idiosyncratic prosodies, icons of mass culture, pictographs, glossolalia, the life of the ghetto.

Third, there has been an impatience with isolated subject matter, the Grecian urn or its homely complement, the red wheelbarrow. For in the century of uncertainty, of mass man and the bombardment of images, one can see the world in a grain of sand only if one simultaneously sees the thousands of undressed oiled bodies baking on the beach, the web of their social interactions, the raw sewage pumped into the sea and the contaminated lives of the marine animals, the kiosks with their pink bunnies and rubber ducks, the thumping transistors and careening frisbies, the bumper-to-bumper traffic snaking along the coast. A macrocosm without microcosm: in the poem all ages are contemporaneous, all events synchronous, each

9

thing is itself and the metaphor of something else. (Metaphor: to move from one place to another. In Greece the moving vans are labelled METAPHORA.)

Fourth, it has meant a criticism of (and despair over) the inadequacy of language: a sense that the poem has lost the language that speaks it, that the poet must either wrestle the language back to (a temporary) meaning or surrender to meaninglessness, perhaps even revel in meaninglessness.

And yet, despite the hopelessness of existing words and forms, the infinity of pressing subject matter and structural possibilities, the poem has retained its ancient identity as an image of wholeness — or more exactly, an image toward wholeness. The 20th century poet is a maker of intricate and beautiful shards who dreams of the golden bowl: not the poem that is, or was, but the poem that should be.

It is a dream that has provoked, among the best poets, a journey. A journey whose path — as there may be no future ahead — can lead only in one direction: back, toward the origins. An uncovering of the past as it lies within, not a nostalgic return. A psychoanalysis of the self and of the species, that the mouth of the snake will finally find its tail, the poem end, and this cycle of history close.

It is of course a mythic and impossible quest. Tragically, it has often led to easy answers: the submission to higher orders (the Church, Eastern or Western; the state religions of Communism and Fascism) or lesser orders (elites, literary movements, reversions to a perceived "tradition"). Often it has led to disorder: the little neuroses, the madnesses and suicides.

An extraordinary poet on this track — and one who has managed to remain resolutely himself — is Clayton Eshleman. No other American poet has gone deeper into human history, personal history, and the body itself. Few have invented, as Eshleman has done, the language to carry him.

A few biographical facts cue the poems:

Ira Clayton Eshleman, Jr., born in Indianapolis, Indiana in 1935, the only child of Gladys and Ira Clayton Eshleman. It was a Middle American childhood as imagined by a West German filmmaker: his father, deacon of the church and efficiency expert at a slaughterhouse; his mother, the meticulous housewife who forbade her son to play with children who were not Protestant and white, whose parents smoked or drank, whose mothers wore slacks. The boy himself is described by the man as "Charlie McCarthy": a well-scrubbed, well-groomed wooden dummy.

The piano became the first window onto a world outside of Indiana. The boy started playing at age seven, gave it up in adolescence to be a jock, then, at 16, discovered bebop: it was the making of a 1950s "White Negro." He entered Indiana University in 1953 as a music major, but switched to business as he became immersed in the world of the Phi Delta Theta fraternity, with its torturers and victims (Actives and Pledges), its Caligulan rites of Hell Week, its saturation bombing of the opposite sex.

In 1957, having bounced in and out of school, he stumbled into poetry,

10

and within a year much of the rest of his life had fallen into place. He edited the university literary magazine, *Folio,* and was in touch with Zukofsky, Creeley, Corman, Duncan, Olson; in New York he met many of the best poets of his generation, all still in their twenties: Rothenberg, Antin, Kelly, Wakoski, Schwerner, Economou, and, of particular importance, the slightly older Paul Blackburn. He hitchhiked to Mexico—his first experience of the rest of the world—and, in the course of bumming around, happened upon a book of César Vallejo's poetry. A year later he was in Mexico again, translating Neruda's *Residence on Earth.* These aspects of the life—Blackburn and Vallejo, magazine editorship, translation, literary friendship, travel to the other worlds—would continue to be central to the work.

He married Barbara Novak in 1961, spent a year in Taiwan, Korea and Tokyo, and two years in Kyoto, teaching English. He returned to Indiana for one last year, and then in 1965 he and Barbara moved to Lima, Peru, where he continued his work on Vallejo and edited an ill-fated bilingual magazine, *Quena,* which was officially sponsored and suppressed for political reasons before the first issue was published. In 1966 his only son Matthew was born, and they returned to the U.S. to live in New York.

The couple soon separated, and Eshleman was deep into the 1960s: the antiwar movement, Reichian therapy, hallucinogens. Affairs with two women, Marie and Adrienne, enter the poetry. In 1967 he founded *Caterpillar,* the major American poetry magazine of the time, which gathered together most of the then-living masters, the young poets of Eshleman's generation, a range of translation from Akutagawa to Artaud, and kindred spirits like Norman O. Brown, Leon Golub and Stan Brakhage.

In 1969 he met Caryl Reiter, his second wife, and in 1970 they moved to Los Angeles, where they still live. Both his parents died the same year. *Caterpillar* ended in 1973, to be reborn eight years later—the fourth incarnation of the Magazine—as *Sulfur.* In 1974 Eshleman began his continuing study of the Paleolithic caves of France and Spain. In 1978, after nearly 20 years of work, his translation of Vallejo's *Complete Posthumous Poetry* was published. Translations of Artaud, Vladimir Holan, Michel Deguy, and the complete poetry of Aimé Césaire have followed since.

An outline of the life is helpful, for the poetry is full of autobiographical specifics, and the progression of Eshleman's major books has closely followed the course of the life: from the first book *Mexico & North* (1962) and its early views of the Third World; to *Indiana* (1964), the poet's childhood and early manhood; *Altars* (1971), an artifact of the 1960's; *Coils* (1973), the synthesis of the earlier books and Eshleman's final coming-to-terms with Indiana; *The Gull Wall* (1975) which breaks out of autobiography to center on Paul Blackburn and a series of personae "portraits"; *What She Means* (1978), an exploration of woman, as incarnated by Caryl Eshleman; and most recently to *Hades in Manganese* (1981) and, his best book, *Fracture* (1983), the poet's descent into the Paleolithic.

It is a poetry that sees the life of the mind, and the meandering path

11

of the work, as a series of imaginative confrontations with the "other"—other humans, other species, the historical other, the geographical other, the personal other. Encounters without resolution: each an act of a continually revised self-definition, as the Indiana Eshleman—the mid-century, Middle American, middle class, white Protestant heterosexual male—sets out to wander in a world that denies every Indiana assumption.

The other humans along this path form a quaternity: the Parents (Ira Clayton & Gladys Eshleman), the Woman/Wife (Caryl Eshleman), the Master (César Vallejo), and the Friend (Paul Blackburn). These are attended by hosts of angels and demons: spirits of creation—Artaud, Van Gogh, Frida Kahlo, Bill Evans, Max Beckmann, Bud Powell, Francis Bacon, among others—and forces of destruction—murderers, torturers, psychopaths. (And typical of Eshleman's work—where each thing flips to its other side—the creative spirits are often victims of self-destruction, the destroyers inadvertent makers of the poem.) Without these others, the I would be the soundless tree falling in the forest: each is a figure of struggle and love, each a mask to be assumed in the stations of the poet's simultaneous dismantling and invention of the ego.

(Here a word should be said of Eshleman's two other primary activities, magazine editing and translation. The magazine: not only a service to the republic and a personal map of the literary landscape, but also a small, selfless participation in the sympathetic work one has not written. As for translation: the dissolution of the translator's ego is essential if the foreign poet is to enter the language—a bad translation is the insistent voice of the translator. Eshleman, in such poems as "The Book of Yorunomado" and "The Name Encanyoned River," presents his long apprenticeship to Vallejo in terms of the lives of the Tibetan saints or of the Castaneda-Don Juan legends: the master Vallejo must break down the disciple Eshleman to come into English; the disciple's ego resists; and ultimately the disciple learns from the struggle his own strengths, the strengths that will aid both the translation and the creation of his own poems.)

The other species are a rain forest of insects and animals, real and imagined; the poems *teem*. Yeats, in *A Vision,* writes of a man who, "seeking an image of the Absolute," fixes on the slug, for the highest and the lowest are "beyond human comprehension." Eshleman, however, in "The Death of Bill Evans," rejects interspecies apartheid to enter into slugness itself, transforming other into brother, finding an animal helpmate as guide to his meditation on the life of the jazz musician. And where many recent poets have resurrected Coyote and other indigenous trickster figures, Eshleman introduces into the poem, in a way that cannot be miscontrued as "pop," the contemporary American trickster, Donald Duck: the final image of the animal at the death of nature.

The geographical other is, in one instance, Czechoslovakia (the suffering of imagination repressed) but mainly it is the Third World: Peru, Southeast Asia, El Salvador, South Africa (the sufferings of poverty and the imperial wars). It is the Morlock-Eloi vision of Wells's *The Time Machine*: Eshleman is one of the few poets to explore, beyond facile polemic, how "Indiana"—the comfort of the American middle-class—is dependent on global misery. He has taken a classic American image—Hawthorne's or Parkman's or Cooper's terrifying "savages" in the dark forest, just beyond the settlement clearing; Poe's or Lovecraft's "unspeakable horror" in the basement of the house—and shown its obverse: we are the cannibals who feed on *them*; our house is *built on* horror.

The invention of the historical other has become almost programmatic in 20th century American poetry: for Pound, ancient China; for H.D., classical Greece; for Olson, Mesopotamia; for Snyder, the Neolithic. Eshleman has pushed the historical back about as far as it can go: to the Upper Paleolithic, and the earliest surviving images made by humans. As a result of his literal and imaginative explorations of the painted and gouged caves, Eshleman has constructed a myth, perhaps the first compelling post-Darwinian myth: that the Paleolithic represents the "crisis" of the human "separating out" of the animal, the original birth and the original fall of man. From that moment, human history spins out: from the repression of the animal within to the current extinction of the animals without; the inversion from matriarchy to patriarchy, and the denial of the feminine; the transformation of the fecund underworld into the Hell of suffering; and the rising of Hell, in the 20th century, to the surface of the earth: Dachau, Hiroshima. The poet's journey is the archetypal scenario of descent and rebirth: he has travelled to the origin of humanness to reach the millennium, end and beginning. In an early poem he had written: "God why has it taken me 31,000 years/ to stand at the threshold?/ Why has it taken 31,000 years to leave home?"

It is Eshleman's confrontation with the personal other that has proved the most controversial. He is, surprisingly, probably the first poet ever to deal, in the poem, with the realities of infancy: not an allegorical "infant joy," but the drooling, babbling selves that are our private Lascaux. More noticeably to his detractors, he has admitted what he calls the "lower body" into the poem: excrement, semen, menstrual blood. This has led the *New York Times Book Review* to sniff, "He will not cooperate with taste, judgment, aesthetic standards . . ." (an essay could be written on that word, *cooperate*!) and an otherwise sympathetic critic to conclude that "Eshleman is not a happy man."

Such response is a bizarre reduction of the poetry to obsessive scatology. One of the main drifts of the century has been the literal re-embodiment of the poem. Thus Williams, in "How to Write" (1936): poetry is "the middle brain, the nerves, the glands, the very muscles and bones of the body itself speaking." Or Olson's "Proprioception" (1962): ". . . that one's life is informed from and by one's own literal body"; "Violence/ knives: anything to get the body in." While it is quite true that the facts of the lower body are prominent in certain Eshleman poems, it is always in context: an implied or apparent yoking with the upper body. It is the "amplitude of contradiction": face and ass, art and shit, menstrual blood and the blood

13

of violence, each turning around and into the other in the poet's "yearning for oneness," the "challenge of wholeness."

Eshleman is the primary American practitioner of what Mikhail Bakhtin called "grotesque realism." It is an immersion in the body; not the body of the individual, the "bourgeois ego," but the body of all: the "brimming over abundance" of decay, fertility, birth, growth, death. Like the collective body, it is unfinished, exaggerated; protuberances and apertures are prominent; animals, plants, objects, the world blend into its undifferentiated and essentially joyous swirl. The mask is its primary device: not as concealer of identity, but as image of each thing becoming something else.

Grotesque realism is "contrary to the classic images of the finished, completed man" (and to the finished, completed poem), "cleansed, as it were, of all the scoriae of birth and development." And it is contrary to what Bakhtin categorizes as "Romantic grotesque": the reaction against classicism which sought to restore the grotesque not in its original celebratory function, but as the malevolent underside of sunny classicism: the opening of the Pandora box of aristocratic gloom, fear, repressed desire and longing for death, where the ordinary "suddenly becomes meaningless, dubious, and hostile."

Eshleman's critics tend to read him in terms of the Romantic grotesque, when his intent has been clearly the opposite. His grotesque is ecstatic and comic; through a systematic shedding of the oppressive weight of national identity and personal biography, he has taken the grotesque beyond Bakhtin's Medieval carnival back to its source: the grotto, the cave. And there he has sought, and partially found, what Bakhtin calls "the complete freedom that is possible only in the completely fearless world."

It is precisely Eshleman's utter fearlessness that scares people off. ("He will not cooperate . . .") No other American poet has laid so much of his life literally on the line. It is illuminating, for example, to read Eshleman's 1970 poem on his father, "The Bridge at the Mayan Pass" alongside such celebrated, nearly contemporary poems as Robert Lowell's "Commander Lowell," Sylvia Plath's "Daddy," Allen Ginsberg's "Kaddish." In the case of Lowell and Plath, it is difficult today to imagine what all the fuss was about. Lowell's poem on his father depends on a safe titillation—the eccentric side of a well-known family—much like his "confessional" poems, which carefully reveal a few autobiographical details shocking to polite society (Mr. Lowell takes tranquilizers, Mr. Lowell was in the bughouse) without saying much at all. Plath has a cloying "more neurotic than thou" machismo; its scandal is a "nice girl" calling her Dad a vampire and a Nazi. Ginsberg's frank autobiography, still startling to read, serves a similar, elitist "band of loonies" function: this is what has made me crazy, this is my admission ticket to the "hipsterheaded angels." Eshleman, however, never wears the proud badge of neurosis. His violent, extremely disturbing rant is intended as a sign of health: the dismantling of the father (and the father in the son) as Indiana, that which denies life. It is an act of making love on the father's freshly-dug grave.

Fearless too is Eshleman's language: dense, gluey, wildly veering from the oracular to the burlesque, strewn with neologisms and weird bits of American speech (*cruddy, weenie, chum, goo*; *tampax* as a verb). An Eshleman poem is unmistakable from the first glance. Image jams against image, not impressionistically, but in the service of a passionately argued line of reason, a line where an idea, before completion, turns into another idea, and then another, much like the walls of the Paleolithic caves. ("Image is cross-breeding/ or the refusal to respect/ the single individuated body.") The poems are nearly impossible to excerpt.

It is surprising that no published critic seems to have noticed that Eshleman is, at times, extremely funny. Where else would one find, in the same poem, Apollo, Persephone, Ariadne and "Silk Booties & Anklets Knit Soaker & Safety Pins/ Hug-me-tight a Floating Soap Dish with Soap Rubber Doggie"? With minor (usually stoned-cute) exceptions, the idea of the comic poem has become so alien to American poetry—who today thinks of Pound as he described himself: "a minor satirist"?—that the poet runs the serious risk of appearing foolish.

It is a foolishness measured by the last vestiges of the distinction between "poetic" and "unpoetic." Wordsworth, despite his championing of the life in common things, went to elaborate lengths in one passage of *The Prelude* to avoid writing the words "tic-tac-toe" (or "naughts and crosses"). To a certain extent that reticence still holds. To bring Rubber Doggies—weird artifacts of the popular grotesque—into the poem's art aerie, to place Francis Bacon and Little Lulu in the same phrase, remains, in poetry at least, an act subversive to "taste, judgment, aesthetic standards." For Eshleman, Little Lulu is the lower half of Francis Bacon's body; to incorporate the two is the work of a comic wisdom.

It is a poetry and a life conceived as a "name encanyoned river" (Eshleman's turn on a Vallejo phrase): a river that springs up in the arid wilderness of Indiana and flows toward a Utopic vision of personal and global wholeness; a river that is nearly all rapids and is flanked by canyon walls. Along the way one writes, paints, leaves one's mark on the walls: both an act of testimony for the community (this is where we are) and an imaginative leap to the other side.

Eshleman's totems for the journey have been the two insect spinners: the spider and the caterpillar. Both draw their art entirely from their own bodies. For one, the web: constructed with astonishing mobility, slung from branch to branch, a net almost all air, through which the world is visible beyond, in which the stuff of the world is randomly trapped. For the other, the cocoon: immobile, opaque, the prison where, in utter solitude, one effects transformation. What better allies could a poet have?

Eliot Weinberger
May 1985

I
THE COASTAL OVENS

EVOCATION I

I walk a fury
of gnats, sun tossing on lake wall
                    Mexican dawn burns, a sorceress across
the waters, circling around me, rising & falling
whipping her veils of menstruated linens
                    odor of earth, damp hay
                    Praise

                    fire & man, men
mounted on rice-field buffaloes, birds
                    singing in the corolla of Chapala
black lily roots lugged in by tubercular kids
hands among oranges, breasts of strong
                    women glistening over
                    rock & hemp

                    my own genitals sweet
as papaya. Lean into wind, see from this
                    balustrade broken steps spilling an
alphabet of stone to the fern groves of Ajijic
beggars unrolling from stairways, a
                    python of backs
                    snailing

                    to the muddy chancel
where St. Anthony is crowned. It is scent of
                    the hunt, of the turned-back coverlet where
with her fingers on the sill of a new day a child is
swept by fog, bellowings of a fresh kill
                    the rain of blackberries
                    on rusted

                    stone
            no seed grows in porcelain
                    bone

1960
Mexico & North

THE CROCUS BUD

The vise of Jung thrills me less than spider

Your fingers even in nightmare find my foot

My hand is never my own unless it can be held

A poetry which throws the entire body into relief

Truth to oneself from which alone fidelity worth-while can come

Poetry a meat tenderizer to break down resistance to my soul

A man who makes love with his wife

Thank god hell is not dead in me

Words stiff bristles to scour sore gums

A Peruvian teething-ring

A Blakean rattle

Song tell her I am in the State of Caterpillar

One yellow crocus in the entire raked grounds

Tell her I can change my life

1962
Indiana

Over coffee, alone

— slowly, surely, they turn
to a crust of biscuit,
nibble a kiss in passing,
koi.
Brothers,
our record changes
nothing

. . . tú, luego, has nacido; eso
tambien se ve de lejos, infeliz y cállate,
y soportas la calle que te dío la suerte . . .

— an interval.
Dangerously, fully, each instant is
a different man.

*

Incredible the force of the Yorunomado coffee-shop. When I first came,
pale sunlight drifted a wide lobby open to a patio where a tiny lantern's
soft red, latticed, glowed. By a dark shield I took a high-backed crimson
chair. A chanson played. Near the patio, a mother and her son sat down.
My word had a painful golden relief, unspoken; it churned, evaporated.
I tried every scheme. I found silence holds only to the music's end. I realized
one must face another. Even if rock, the other is a garden. Incredible the
scroll pressed out and held by four hands; on the table a letter from Bashō,
Le Pont Mirabeau. I had faith in a deadend, in dignity, and delight. The
Yorunomado coffee-shop compounded a language of man.

*

and in the shallow pool by my feet
thin vermilion *koi*
motionless
love
grows and spends in me

*

Like flame fleshed, voices
shoot about over the mossy stones. A foot down:
Europe shimmering light, Paris with the intensity of heat waves.
But this brick wall. This crude clay
no matter how much I want to wander out, to be a crimson pennant
unfurling in a blackening spired sky—
this hand of bloodsmeared Indiana wall . . .
O dimension of love I had imagined, O
structure in which, though terror drained, no energy was lost . . .

Flame torn, voices roil in compounding fire, the sea
—no. From this iron
chair: a pool of *koi*. Rose-popsicle
gold; plucked-chicken pink
with a pus-yellow head; and one a dream, the smoky purple
the moon gives to the otherwise midnight . . . *The Four Zoas*—
a new life. Floating on the surface, the mung
he took into his mouth:

                    perfected
            far off,
                a gong

My language is full of dirt and shit.

Is it too great a leap to imagine
rice may spring from these waters,
                        a yellow
                    carp, a green carp?
—over there, still
under the knobby lotus, she with the white-splashed red belly,
pregnant, who is she?

        *

What demand. I am
blind as the bat-
god. There is nothing I can do.

She bleeds
and my silkworm eats a half-moon in the mulberry leaf

She bleeds
and now I get her want

22

The word is not enough
nor is grief.
Walking down the hospital steps—

WHAT was never born?

    *

Paused on the Shichijo Bridge,

       the day misty,
lovely, grisly . . . the Kamogawa fades, shallows forever,
winding out through Kyoto's southern shacks . . .

       below, in the littered mud,
a man stabs around in cans and sewage,
in his ragged khaki overcoat and army puttees
I was taken forward to a blind spot

       (he pulled himself up
a rope ladder hung over the stone embankment
and with limp burlap sack slung over his shoulder
disappeared down an alley
home? to the faces?
          What do
I express when I write?
  Knives?   or Sunlight?
          And everything
that lives is holy raced through my mind

       Walking home,
paused under the orange gates of Sanjusangendo, in
under the dripping eaves, cosy,
I noticed a strand of barbwire
looped over stakes I had stepped
inside of

       and then it came to me)
       I would kill for you

THE DUENDE

Overcast, after lunch, the sky fled. A colorless darkening void. The
neighborhood still. Walking, there was a light behind my head. At

the corners of my eyes it fuzzed into cold obscurity. I must molt more than my face. As if these brown houses, this standing alley water, were the only reality. I must change more than the contour of my line.

It should be that the slightest scar of moss on the rainstreaked fence occasion delight. And an old man, squatting on his steps, wringing out a rag, praise. And when the man in my mind smiles, children should fill the alley, white clouds drift high in the bright blue heavens over Tsuruginomiya.

When the female principle takes over, it has been said that it is The Darkening of the Light. Likewise, as has not been said, it is the point at which, recrossing Shichijo Bridge, I picked up from the embankment stone a slightly fishy, sweet, urine smell: the scent of Vallejo—

from which I learned: everything I sense is human, at the very worst *like a man.* And—that which can darken is not without light. Faint along the back of the emptiness grazes the herd of the multi-chambered sun.

> I entered Yorunomado and sat
> down, translating,
> *Nightwindow.*

> The coffee breathed
> a tiny
> pit—

As a black jeweled butterfly alights
in late summer on a hardening coil of dung,
so I lit on his spine

pages lifting in the breeze   in from the patio

We locked. I sank my teeth into
his throat, clenched, his fangs
tore into my balls, locked
in spasms of deadening pain we turned, I
crazed for his breath, to translate
my cry into his gold, howling, he
ripped for food

Locked, a month passed, and as he increased lean
I slackened, drained, and tripling my energy

24

drew blood, not what I was after, muscles
contracting expanded he was clenched
in my structure, turning
substance, a dead matter
eating into my cords, and saw deep
in his interior a pit, in spring
I went for it, made myself into a knife
and reached down, drawing
out from the earth cold.
A hideous chill passed—

another month, cunningly
he turned himself into a stone

I dulled on, grinding my own teeth, woke up,
another month, a season. I was wandering
a pebbled compound, the stone in hand.

I saw I had birthed the deadend, but Japan
was no help—until I also saw
in the feudal rite of *seppuku* a way.

On the pebbles I lowered stonelike.
Whereupon the Spectre of Vallejo raised
before me: cowled in black robes, stern on the *roka*,

he assumed a formal kneel. With his fan
he drew a bull's-eye on my gut;
he gave no quarter; I cut.

Eyes of father tubes of mother swam
my system's acids. As one slices raw tuna
with shooting contortions not

moving a foot I unlocked Yorunomado
from the complex cavework of my own tomb.
Vallejo kept his word:

he was none other that one year than himself

Hello all I have ever felt . . .

for this was the point upon which the pen
twisted loose an ego
strong enough to live.

Set in motion, the servants
washed down and raked the pebbles.
Deepening shadows, they crossed and recrossed,
swinging smoking braziers, chatting.
One, grizzled, picked up a lopped topknot,
grinned, and dropped it in the pail.
Far off, in the interior of this strange place,
a quiet weeping was heard.
Although who cut and who condemned were one,
the weeping was too sincere to be that of a lord.
In the heart of the poem there was
no longer a hesitation before power.
The platform on which the stuff was cut and shaped,
this very platform holds the life of another.

"Will you help me?"

I turned away and wrote:
*I am taking a walk and holding Barbara's hand, a field
slower than centuries we've no mind of*

But Vallejo insisted: "NO. LA MANO, HE DICHO."

You struggled up sinking
between your elbows, braced,
and turned eyes
were a miscarried woman.

Standing, I reached
under the arched wall of your back
and eased in under you
the bedpan.

Leaving the moist warmth of your back,
I sat down, your shattered dream
no longer divided from mine.

*

Entering me then the pebble of bread he put into his mouth, softly pass-
ing through my face the point of Vallejo, the trench and glory of his human
face, in my lips his, alum dry, passed, and with them my desire to die.
The yanked-tight viscera loosened, gave, it opened a palm for the bread
and cupped, a flower parched, opening, closing, a dark red flower moving

with heaven's untiring power, the verb coursing raggedly, wild at first, then gentle, beating, whereupon the sutra went into motion, dark monotone moving horizontal through the twilit bass, syllable upon syllable compounding, whereupon the compound-complex went into motion with the simple following close behind — I felt the line set, and from the right flow back into me through the fire rushing out to you from the left, from margin to margin, mingling, ripening, the flow knelt and prayed in my breath, it swept through my seat and cling, kissing my heart on its wing it cleansed, coiled, unfurled

1964
other versions
in *Poetry* (Chicago),
Indiana and
Coils

And Yorunomado stood in the howling bay, waves
lash & wail into the booming caverns; he looked
to where the ovens were lit walls & the Sons of
the Sepik Delta worked in flaming reds & blacks;
O Gladys Enter! he cried to the shadow at his side,
Enter the ovens & be transmuted to my wife. Or forever
die, no longer plague me with what I can't see, for I cannot
worship the root, I cannot carry the taro through the lines
of relation. No longer is Coatlicue visible
but there is a woman enfibered in my veins, a hot
wet in my hand I have been told, I recall is you.
And here you stand, a writhing molten red, a
beckoning mush to maintain me always to the fork
& spear, in housemother agedness, while the victims
trembling holding hands are made to bend over as before
the mask was built, naked young men holding hands bent
over encircling the blazing center, a double fireplace;
"Slaughter on 10th Avenue" is picked from the shelf;
where a Phi Delt pin was fixed through a sweatered breast
into a padded bra, the furniture has been set aside,
the revelation of her armor & chastity is at hand, the victims
chatter & sob, the semen begs release—snuck out
in the crematorial lavatories it sobs to witness the flames;
the rites of passage deep-freezed her armor keeps them im-
potent, they stand being victims to be masters later! The hi-fi
needle is lifted, the lights turned low, the corral-gate bursts,
the Sons of the Sepik Delta shoot out bouncing and roaring from
their brides; only a few are not broken; I am shouting faint
with disbelief from the negation of life that is Indiana "O holy
Generation, Image of Regeneration!" The virgin wife discovers
on her wedding night the spur marks in the sides of her
little husband! She turns on in secret fury! Enter O
Enter the ovens that I may love you! Be transmuted to
my kind, invisible, for I am in great error, a part of a great
& terrible error, I must go to Eternal Death. Even as I speak
the Sons dress up in swastika red & gather grinning to my left,
the ideals of art wait patiently to my right.

Whenever any Individual
Rejects Error & Embraces Truth, a Last Judgement
passes upon that Individual.

Yorunomado knew
he had found his wall, for looking down
he saw his thighs emblazoned moons,
his ankles suns, a starry midnight-
blue painted as if on clay across
his gut. He felt his universe flex
as he moved more openly across the beach;
he had taken upon himself self-enclosing
divine attributes; on North Jordan
he had passed judgement on a girl from Anderson;
in Chapala he had mocked a woman hungry for marriage—
but how not mock? The natural sexual
activity has become anathema to man;
whom he faced across the sand was none
other than himself in any other woman
or man, & to act upon them was to act
upon himself, a vicious self-perpetuating
doubt, & in the arms of the Sons of the Sepik
Delta he felt the vein of Gandhi, a pure
stream in India, but he could not mock
the presence with whom he lived,
and he remembered Jung's words:
The source of life is a good companion.

He looked hard around him on the beach
at the sea & at the sky. Were not all these grains
placed by abstinence? Is not *everything* sand,
the tree, the house, a friend's lips, a bird, a
sunbeam, when creation is overruled by a truth?
There is in the life of every man & woman a moment
Origin's watchfiends cannot find, that moment
settles on various pins, it may be at any
place & must be taken there, & he knew he
was really dealing with desire, that that "moment" was
the moment of desire, & if that moment is
denied, the rest of the day is dead.

So did he attempt to understand the Last
Judgement he was in the process of,
now he knew the intorsions of *seppuku,*
that who he fought to emerge was not
just a spectre, Gladys wailed in the cry
of every passing gull but she was not
his enemy, only he could be transformed
in the coastal ovens, signs were everywhere

but there was something he was missing
to make these signs cohere . . .

Forgiveness & self-annihilation were
surely signs, but in what act? He continued
walking. Sea. Sand. Sky. No
thing lived or moved . . .

Distant down the beach he saw a bench,
or a raised structure behind which
something moved; on 2 x 4s a box, a
casket from which a tattered
winding sheet fluttered. He approached
fearfully for he knew who was in the box
but not who moved behind it; he approached
the casket of Vallejo as a book is closed,
toward the heavy box of flesh blowing
by the sea, seeing a man crouched
moving behind, who he feared was himself.
Los stood naked with his hammer behind
the casket of Vallejo smiling at Yoru-
nomado; he put his hand upon the beaten
lid as the wanderer approached, smiling,
for he alone knew what I must do, & he stepped
back as I knelt by the box in dignity, in prayer
to Vallejo. Los stood & watched,
& Yorunomado saw how those who weep in
their work cannot weep, how those who
never weep are the weak, the fake
sufferers. To be a man. That suffering
is truer to man than joy. These were
the lines in the heavy pocked face of
Vallejo, trinities of intersections &
heavy lines, a village of nose & lids;
Vallejo never left home, it was home
he always begged for even in the taking on
of the suffering body of man. I stood for
7 years & looked at him there, ob-
serving the Quechuan rags & shreds of
priestcloak, the immense weight in his mind,
& lifting his rags I saw his female gate,
bloodied & rotten, hopelessly stitched
with crowfeathers, azure, threaded with
raw meat, odors of potatoes & the Andes,
& how the priestroaches had gotten into
the gate, yet the edges of his gate were

30

sewn with noble purple velvet & I pondered
my own course, what was in store for me
given the way I was living, how the female
gate in a man must open, yet the horrible
suffering if it opens & something else does
not open! But there was no cure or cause
for who Vallejo was, perhaps it was the enormity
of what he took on, the weight of his people
to utter, & I shuddered to think of Indiana,
of what it would be to cast Indiana off.
Yorunomado sobbed when he saw the extent
of contradiction in Vallejo's body, how
could he have lived even one day, he thought;
this was the agony in the lines, the fulness
& the dark beauty of Vallejo's face horizontal
to sky, long black hair flowing back
into the sand, & Los likewise moved bent
& rested his hammer for one day in tribute
to the fierce & flaming profile contoured
to the horizon . . .

How long had he been left there? Yorunomado
stood & with Los helped the casket off
into the sea of another language. How long
Vallejo had been there! His winding sheet
was entangled with digging sticks & scrapers;
they set the casket on fire & left it blazing
to the shore water. They waded back,
& their hands were streaked with flesh,
their legs covered with veins, in the
hollow of their crab-like chests
a heart was hung, cock & balls swung
between their thighs. They knew
what Vallejo heard

beating beating beating the seas of misery beat upon the shore
& the roll in is a woman trying for a man
& the roll back is a man fleeing from a woman
& the million grains are children the waves beat upon
& the men walk in the women & the women walk in the men
but this is hidden to most by the very laws most have made up
Each sand is an eye Yorunomado is an eye of God
Every day every man ascends Niemonjima
for Niemonjima is the arising the going forth
& every night every man descends Niemonjima

for Niemonjima is the hill the walking down to sleep
& Yorunomado prayed: be patient with me my friends,
nothing is to be held back.

1965
Coils

WALK VI

Walked again over Santa Rosa Bridge—
when I worked for the North American Peruvian Cultural Institute,
I could see a cross-topped hill from Sponholz's
office—highest of poor grassless
hills in & about Lima—

SAN CRISTOBAL HILL—How will the Institute look
from the base of your cross?

Through Almeida—a carnival of stalls
on concrete (where
must the discharge go?)   High iron fences—
maids dozing in park grass (not
a romantic image here)   Statues (another
age)   I turned in but was rebuffed—
"Private—The Water Passage, what you want, is
around there—"
                    another dead end with poor come
out to look—
                    below the pink convent wall, a dry
viaduct—The Water Passage—I started to climb

the work is carrying water—I saw many faces
come out & didn't think to say Good Morning—the poor
unsettle me, degenerate the poem—it seems a structure
holds only *against them*—one is always carrying one's
sun—a smoking brazier—& walking fast—called
to the murderer's attention—out to look for shit—for
the first of the stations.

Passed by trucks carrying water—
the work is   what? Not to quit a poisoned
job—is
the battle—Arjuna. Is facing one's task—
first station of the cross.

is shuffling up this hill—the stations
meaningless, politics a horrible excuse (in the sense
that any, or no, choice kills)

thought a roofless shack —
the image without water —

                                        A starving woman selling razor-
                                        slices of rotten watermelon
                                        —eyes bugged—
running down the road past me as if she were on the last
bend of a 440 — I'm the Institute
going up —

        House unpainted 50 feet away —
up close worse — gangrene hill — before a shack
a pile of ripe mahogany crawling with flies —
death can be more alive than life —
Roman numerals gouged in waist-thick station posts —

    At the top of the world are pigs
rooting in human garbage.
Overlooking Lima — 8 bolgias abstract — this
night abstract —
        & I've never meant more to say what I mean.
Shacks disappear at the level of only stone — last image:
pigs,
        heaped refuse, kids names on rocks —
an hour of last images.   The new "vivienda"
worse than the Cantagayo slum — pipeline of gas chambers
fitted out in shadowless valley —

        to go in — to cure —
or as Rothenberg put it: "Sometimes I'd rather be shaman"
and I: "then the life's not in the work"
                —here pulled to pig's *Test of Poetry*

writing with a little stick on rock
expressionless face of nature
what else is a cross?   San Cristóbal's is 30 feet tall
                        studded with giant lightbulbs, both
                        post & beam packed with them —
                        at the base a generator grinds away

Barbara   Clayton   No love is forever:
the source of this sea of emotion? To be
        on top — see that cross
lit nightly over killer Lima — over the sleep
of thousands of foetalhoods like mine
            what meaning this dove over world?

34

To write with a stick in rock dust on rock.
quarries of sunlight—road now to 10th station

art a repercussion   10 layers above starvation

1965
Walks

MATTHEW'S BIRTH

This son who's appeared to us
passed & has yet to come—
    blue, swaddled in bloody linen
the supermarket cart paused,
I looked (big balls, screaming
appendages in the form of claws)
    Matthew Craig Eshleman
    you've been born into a deceitful world.

Who split us apart as a tree
    has yet to appear human:
the man in the doctor who promised
I could watch the birth—the woman
in the nun who backed the doctor's
betrayal—I hugged you & felt what
    pain I could—& saw your
    profile—Greek warrior—
      I felt your urine & wanted

sight of my child that is yours—
beautiful woman from whom has
    transferred all my gold—
what broke us apart for our son's glory
    is this world we are in—
    product of my luminous salts!

It was **THEN** I saw man alive a son of a bitch, a son
of a bitch born, son of a bitch dead
a son of a bitch dying—
Naturally Vallejo is sore—
naturally Luvah will burn in his furnace,
Vala howls, & what is not seen
are your meats naturally red
grape, blood, magenta azalea & pine—
beauty of resistance! Who held terror
in her teeth this afternoon must suffer
my hurt! Dachau I've never
lived in! Godmother of my unexplained
faults! The hair of my son in your dilated vagina

was your hair I took in my teeth—
& your look, forgiving all, what I
can't make now—what I wasn't allowed to see.

1966
Walks

THE 1802 BLAKE BUTTS LETTER VARIATION

Saturday noon I walked out of my home
to Holcomb Gardens, a mile or so through
the Butler Woods where I found a moist
rubber during the Second World War,
around the pond, down path under a hornet's nest
& to the canal, heavy
for Barbara & Matthew seemed
gone, the bend always in sight,
leaves floated crisp autumn's
first waters,
        the canal
Speed Hubbell's little brother
Pete was dragged from — in lunch line
"did you hear?" Drowned.
  I was carrying Wilhelm Reich.
    Heavy brown canal
that always in my mind has rocked
like a boa within itself, easing
slowly around Dead Man's Drop
where I sledded successfully at
12,
    in noon haze sunlight
misting canal
         all things pass —
learn from dropped leaves & little
Pete
      This is the culmination of 5
years together
      She is buried here.
If you grasp & cling to this sorrow
its wingéd life you'll destroy
        Sodden in my chest
I sat by the bank
All my poetry to now
a wall through which I've tried
entrance, but nevertheless a wall
Book thrown up to shield me from another's sight
  How can you turn from your
mother's eyes? How can you not
feel emotion with Barbara?

                    I got up & started across
Holcomb Gardens, a nave of grass
between wilted beds leading to an artificial pond—
    no, it was blue with water
I was wrong, & guided over by Persephone's
first steps from hell,
autumn's green shaded her bronze
shoulders, bare to waist
                              gown
loose about her.

    I was afraid to let my imagination
lead—I wanted to recount all

Persephone opened herself
& was leading *me* from hell,
I was following her lit taper
through the sewer of the canal
but as I touched her gown strings
I heard Barbara groan behind
& Matthew wailing in a cloud
& my mother set her foot against the canal & start to cross
& my father a wingèd ant begging in his own house
    I opened my breast   full of maggots
& as I began to pull them out
a stench of piss & dust blinded my eyes
    but the beggar was only melodramatic,
I continued march,
reorganizing from a seed to follow out . . .

                    to lead across
my mother? Return home & feed
my father? Leave Matthew
in a cloud & Barbara buried alive?

I was wrong, the day was blue with water
I found a stone bench
Again tried to read what I knew was true
but the truth was beside the point.

I have put knowledge over love
I have broken a heart to avoid my own destruction
I have not given my life for another
I have said
    I will live only for myself
for only then

can I live
And this is in contradiction to the teaching of my master:
Jesus spoke to Albion:
"Fear not: unless I die thou canst not live:
"But if I die I shall rise again & thou with me.
"This is Friendship & Brotherhood: without it Man is Not."
And I heard Barbara groan 40 feet
below in the mud & Matthew weeping from his cloud.
Again I tried to read
again I tried to nostalgize my father & my mother,

    I thought of Blake
kicking the Thistle,
breaking the back of that which
stood in his road
& how another, Vallejo, simply
sat on the Thistle.
    But no other man's way
obtains when there is no one to be seen
   & I wandered among the warm fruit trees,
in the grass among the benches
   & the sky sagged full of Matthews
& the ground churned with the helpless
choke of self-pity

    for Barbara was in New York City
& clouds streamed across the heavens
for Matthew is with Barbara in New York City
& Persephone a statue, a form
my mind took to reach from hell
     & I shook the tree
O God, why has it taken me 31,000 years
to stand at the threshold
Why has it taken me 31,000 years to leave home?

1966
Indiana

THE YELLOW GARMENT

You were the girl
who wanted to serve
devoted
       K'un

  in a yellow garment.
who have not allowed your light to
shine forth,
living quietly
doing the best you can

         one of the oldest images we have of
woman
   "the dark force possesses beauty but veils it"
the man rends it
    again & again she veils it
         her hair helps

to serve
to take care of me

       "it is the way of the earth to make
no display of completed work but rather to bring
everything to completion vicariously"

but I do not want a vicar

I must risk bringing myself
—knowing that what is complete cannot endure—
to completion by
myself
    alone.
        Even tho I fear
the earth is right
    since I so much believe in the earth
it must be right

     You were the girl
I chose
who came along, without resisting,

when I took you by the hand
that in itself is so beautiful

       Who wanted to serve
& still do
         & who I have now pushed
bowl
    away from my hand—

    The girl in a yellow garment
tears in her eyes before her King, saying
"But it is good food I have made you—
I myself am good
as an apple is good

    & here is Matthew
who is an apple too

& you have taken us
& cast us on the earth

where will we go?
what will we do?"

1967
Indiana

DIAGONAL

You walk away across
6th Avenue
lean shoulders
yang stride in
short red skirt
Diagonal
   as on a roadsign
I am alone
— with you
or not,
I am alone
     As I was
a day in Kyoto
the earth
thundered under
my feet,
a roadsign
in the pour
   Coiling red arrow
                  as
certain
   as your diagonal
away — only then
it was my father
beat in my chest
   had manifested his
presence as you
now, as certainly,
are fixed
     Diagonal   that should
I start the other way
    Crossing
would be our death.

   Perhaps it is my
archetype for woman
is a Circle,
that I must sense
ring in the water
to wholly love
anyone —

           that seems
so thin,
yet what is there beyond
such counters
to express
     the mutable sign I am.
                         I feel
I've been at this poem
for centuries
You lay me open
& I sing
You lock me
I am   oak
     flayed into stripes
skunk
     & with that force
I divide in four
men,
     headhunters on a log
Eight eyes as I climax
in you
     Split in four
like a table,
     as if to say
it's my nature
to fear your blood
          depict you
Iron Maiden
          — I am that iron
in which a man is locked
& you cross 6th Avenue
while it pours in the New
Guinea I am,
     terrified at the thought
of being alone —
     & absolutely calm.

And here I am, talking
about Marie
or was it
Coatlicue
     or a stone.
Not who I am
but where.
how.

                    It seems I can
not be naked
to you — not ever
touch you
with the tenderness
I touch my son.
What is
            touching you?
Four headhunters
on a log
    I go crazed
before you
You
sob into the stone
        Diagonal
which is the sun
        Diagonal
the slant that is always leaving
sesgo of the egg
    as it curves
& keeps on curving
& as you slant home
    curve on to New Jersey
to the England you're always leaving
                    As if it won't end
but always is
which is the end
    we call being in the present

watermelon
cherry
whipped cream
nose piece
thrust
    of your trust in me
as you align yourself
over my body
    More vulnerable than a man
can ever be
    but without needing the tremendous
mobility I need to move
through
cherry
fear
Wheatstone's

bridge
    to contact.

Mile
razor
telescope
palm
    over my
inheritance of 8 eyes,
    · O great spider that you are,
slung
    in the skull of a world
I call blue sky!
        To make the inheritance
present.
    To be at your diagonal
which is your definition
siren down 6th
        which is simply sound

as you are simply spirit

hung with a nosegay of blood.

1968
Indiana

SOUTINE

for Nora Jaffe

The smell of shit
holy Smilovitchi
wholly Indianapolis
our child yoked
one membrane
slaughterhouse
pigment
the hunger of paint
the hunger of the vacant dinnertable
parents' eyes like empty plates
my plate was filled
potatoes weenies milk
his plate was filled
shtetl shtetl shtetl
pigment in the ox
pigment in her hand
ooze of the first semen
slaughter menstruation
to make a vagina is to paint
poem a vagina made in a man
cut me the boy cries
transport over the back of
an elder
      this is an elegy
end of the old rite.
from now on you are to make it my
pigment told me way
  of survival
thru art

   *

is way of survival is Smilovitchi
Indianapolis art the passage
        what
we never saw,   I never saw them kill
my father worked next to the wall against
whacked bullhead 30 feet up encased red
brick accountant
      fowl,   I never saw them twist

the neck of my dinner is way of survival
rite de passage is Smilovitchi
                    is Indianapolis
trees,   I was too frustrated to
look at a tree,   still-life,   world in reel,
his bouquets flowers six feet stalks bright
flags of blood tossing buoys,
midnight   his
midnight in the closed shop
a white fowl hangs
corruscated bag of jewels
dripping from cenote,   virgin,   he never saw the
virgins in my poems.   how
can my poems influence him now that he is dead.
he is not dead.
he is a flower.
    I walk into the garden, pick a lemon, smell
cut it into my soup
our talk this talk no more than birdchitter
cut it into your soup
art act
I slit my throat into my soup
I eat the breast of Soutine
amalgam
amalgam,   of one man
   the world is not a lie our
child told us,   love.
                 imperative
                      love this
greater-than-you
for me to spread open the beef,
see a vagina in every rock
for him to eat, race against
Talmudic law, as goldfish race against
our heart, magnolias a tablecloth
room in dizziness, in state of gesture as a flower
I am in my pigment like in my body
body I've tried so hard to get out of
as he, and so hard to get
in to the body, impossible amalgam
is art.

1968
Indiana

48

THE OVERCOATS OF EDEN

In less than the pulsation of an artery it
is altered —
          where you were was suddenly
not — you stood
by her tub
her word to you
you allowed, put
you in Eden —
               you entered not
to free her, but for
company —
          knowing you were dead you wanted you
picked her up you
danced with her you
thought not of freeing her nor
yourself you
longed to get one
thing straight
               you
saw the possibility of
a poem, you
danced with her you
demanded to pick her up
(pick him up) you
demanded to speak with
the King (the
Queen) You told her
the greatest thing can
happen between us is

a child She told you (He
No, it's Us (She
actually, then: orgasm is
the best thing can happen
between us,
          jogging in Max's
Kansas City you
shouting No
it is a child She No
it is an orgasm
               You

walked her home
You walked,
her home. She
(He
walked
beside you (You
invited you're In
now in this filthy
(the red rags around
her (His
legs, 31
feet under ground
a little bowl placed
under the bars held
rice, you ate that thinking,
you wanted to masturbate in
her, That
She (He
said was alright (So she
ate His cock there A
servant it seemed placed
strangled by your ear
Forced jetty

the dream opened
a summer house with
all your relatives was
Grand Central Station on
the front porch your father as
you rummaged at her
clothes, delightful moustache
40, his age when you
were born, Come on in
(at the rim of her bathtub
morning What do you do
when you are alone?
                    Why I
masturbate (entered in that word
the roundhouse of all the peoples of
the earth refracted of
course 50 prisms say, visible
reunion (stuck
with the ball & streamers, but
Then He taking you through the Aunts
& Uncles to

Your Mother! What sweetness now!
How lovely to have life moving at
the gait of the poem! That seemed
your mother (He disappeared
sprung upon you as your life
with the other relatives (Esh
leman Little Ash Tree outside
And then my mother & I, she
now in her motherform, were in back
yard under the family tree summer
here winter Adrienne now Caryl
Our conversation is a lovely fucking
I mean my mother was a spider
We were going up & down in her
(His web She (not
how to instruct me (
blank shot the pride
blaze but that's ok
you're in the only place you'll
ever be it's personal I mean it's
sexual the tree that curves before
You just can't step outside this or
the tree is America — O
that's what you were telling me O
this tree with the bathtub in its roots
Is what happens when I walk down the street
What street your head This son is
What I wanted to tell you Adrienne
Ariadne but since you can hear me it's
not just a dream & my mother & I were
Under my voice it rolls along my feet
Through the ground Is there a distinction
She, was asking, Do You (He
understand now We'd better go back
Daddy wonders where we are
(but the bright gladiators I cautioned
Here, you can touch it, that's
fury, you'd just better rip up that sheet
You're drunk now in the heart of the poem
But I was just walking down (He
was off talking to the relatives (The
Relatives, the Puns, What fun so I
did that little wincing walk down the aisle
splashing & splashing & splashing Was
it just you wanted to see your Father &
(Him, No I wanted (He

ah, to live a little Not to be locked out
Ah we'd better go back your Daddy's
a drunk boat roacking & roacking
ok—my pain is about done I'll die soon so
We'd better go back to Him (red rags
but is that my father a piece of shit (She
now lost under (He was talking Aunt Ivy
I mean Uncle Charles how beautiful Indiana
outside of America is (the chains on Angela
Davis like a campus lies of course you want
She's a part of you (I wonder How father did
you know her (well I had rheumatism at 18 then I
started to play the cornet O
I understand now how you feel No
wonder we're under the banister
it's ok to get inside like this without
surface, ah they're gonna be awful mad
at you talkin like this, I know Dad, but
this was how our talk was you know you
never spoke To me I know the poem is only
inside (He What you wanna do Split my
Head no this joke is very serious You
Must not blow up the pen
How did we get here Well you Fell
Can't we leave now No I have that old
car in which you always wanted to ride
O I thought you were Caryl no just a body you
swear fidelity now? Of course to you since
You're me sleeping but I'm awake Of
course you are you're sitting in this chair
You mean if everybody were to do this Yes
(He ho ho ho (& then Aunt Iva not Ivy but ivA
that was your grant him her You won
Jesus my father how nice to taste your seamless
Grant Get in, it's an old car a buggy won't
take us Far That's a number Get in
I just wanted to ride a while listen to my
poem sink into its manure O that's (SheWe
weewee rode along little droplets down I
just waking walked with a hardon out of sleep
What do you do when you (bumping down that
countryroad My father & I to get a beer O
yes with Robert & Denis bumping down night
but the town was closed (HeShe absolute
fern wrath overcoats the people in overcoats
They were like trees the Town

the beerhalls closed only little lights
But that's my dream my father said Just
it is Just to ride with you 60 or so years
O well I was turning to Caryl now in Adrienne
Who are they Well you can't now know Since
the Trees of Eden had on overcoats Well
it's beautiful you're out of America (O i

1970
Coils

ODE TO REICH

Wilhelm for you I would sit in the reverberation of The Last Supper
& still keep my eyes to the gentle look in the eyes of children,
for you I would make love to Caryl
would keep her as the vent through which I experience the world,
for you I would make her the terminal,
the station in which all the trains unload
with girls upon girls upon girls & fathers & old men & mothers,
for you, I would keep her before me, keep
that need of the unknown unknown through her,
& known in the rain that falls on me, in that sopping bed the poem
    is
alone in the landscape that you almost alone inhabit
We love & embrace in a lone bed set out in a meadow
Nearby a city of fire

Wilhelm four years I have watched you alone this century
kindling the heavens over that lone meadow bed,
four years I have watched you daily rub off the soot from Baudelaire's
immortal lines: "Real civilization consists not in gas,
not in steam, nor in turning tables, but in the diminution of
the traces of original sin."
                          Concerned doctor, in work pants &
work shirt, in the photo I have of you page 173 in your *People In*
    Trouble
1934 in Sweden, in exile then in the full flow of your Arean arrow
sprung from the bow of your breeding laboratory for butterflies when
you were 10, your ax-head Arean profile looking intently then 37 at
something we know off the page,
                          in the page of the youth breathing
fully for the first time in his life on a cot you in the late 20s
moved around from the chair placed behind him to sit
beside him, look him in the eyes & not use his dreams but confront
    him,
you are in a meadow in a room, yes! with insects buzzing in the dry
rigid prone youth on a cot on a hillock, you are torridly maintaining
his emotions are an expression of his biology & that his biology is
expression of a cosmic energy, that
We love & embrace in a lone bed set out in a meadow
Nearby a city of fire

Wilhelm four years, but the count is for all men, four years Blake
with marginalia on Lavater, this like an advance on Baudelaire:
"But the origin of this mistake in Lavater & his contemporaries
is, They suppose that Woman's Love is Sin; in consequence all
the Loves & Graces with them are Sins." —you Wilhelm
making rain over these lines, scouring them from reason,
keeping the fine edges cut into stone sharp in man's infinite
times of trouble, in work pants & work shirt (this image is
very important)—your compassionate eye on Merton
soundlessly repeating his rounds in the circumscribed nature of
Trappist, Kentucky, speaking gently to him in your fury of
your text on Jesus: "The great mistake is not the curbing of
man's evil urges for free-for-all-fucking with dead genitals,
the great mistake is the burying of the very natural powers in
man's body which alone are capable of putting out of function
the perverted sex in mankind."
    God, Wilhelm, what a tract your
arrowhead everywhere would lead me to, how difficult it is to
move you into the company of poets where for all centuries you
belong, there is so much cause, so much argument, so many
things to set straight; you with the medieval strangeness of
your simple frank theories, your orgone accumulator like a gigantic
slingshot before the Castle, your hollow metal pipes bringing
rain down on dubious Tim Reynolds visiting a farmer in Michigan,
Tim told me "I didn't believe he could make rain, he held the
pipes up to the bright sky and then we went in and drank beer,
it suddenly poured, an hour and when we left, a few miles away
the sun was again shining!"
    To call you a poet
     is to deepen your place as an advance on
imagination, it is not to say you are not a doctor nor to slant
you so as to keep anyone from your meaning as a scientist;
it is the revolution of the identity of a person & his expression,
as such to make for Harry Lewis morality a function of intuition,
that these are not separable things, you urge me tonight
in a bar in New York City—as Breton felt Fourier in a fresh
bunch of violets at the foot of his statue in Paris, I feel you
before me in an unknown girl, she is your bunch of violets Wilhelm,
this girl in her voluptuous body & pretty face hard
with what you call "armoring" sipping brandy & wondering
What is my life? She came in her confusion to
enter the poem, for I would rather not go to Maine to stand
before your tomb, but allow her as the living violet to
enter the poem and say Yes—
I feel you most next to me in Caryl &

I feel you before me as emanation of something not
mine, and in this very wood bench
your imagination vibrating violets
at the foot of your statue which is
now at Vallejo's cross in the Andes
& in Baudelaire's prayer that he simply might be able to work
& in Breton's old manifestoed hand in New Mexico
writing his *Ode to Fourier,* these saints
poets recognize in their own trembling energies to be
Jesus in their own hearts, that pioneering
cosmic fateful strength we know of you
through Aries, your glyph in the pulsating zodiac of
expansion contraction, the body of man
you as a red red Mars come like Isaiah
out of the judgement of the wine vats of your own being,
you curved, as your arrow was not wont to curve, you
bent the drive of that arrow, how can I say it, — to bions,
to heat sand once you had seen what drove you, to
keep the thing out of system, to follow out the strange
crooked road, to keep moving outward, & to keep perception
vital, to not backtrack in your later years & smudge
what I shall call your *clarification of Beulah.*

                                    Wilhelm, what I am
getting at is to somehow honor the clarification you
gave us of self-sacrifice, that the substance of love is
kept fresh in the death of feminine form, this happens in
that meadow, in the giving up of pride & possession, of
man & woman allowing their bodies to convulse, to dissolve
truly thoughts & fantasies, this is the sacrifice Blake named
Eternal Death, to die there in joy with another, that that form
die, that the substance be liberated to find fresh form in
creation. We love & embrace in a lone bed set out in a meadow
Nearby a city of fire
our brother William Blake named Eden, is creation &
in your understanding of the creative process you embrace
the poets telling them
sexual hindrance is imaginative crippling,
how simple you now appear, shoveling the hate out of our bodies,
you sturdy, in your work pants, with no mantle, no egg to
balance on your shoulders, you gazing intensely at
Vallejo's cross in the Andes on which you forever see
"Until I labor I in labor lie"
explaining to him in the ruins & dust that Beulah allows
the transmission, that creation is

not that struggle with the body,
that poetry is translation not just of language
but the passing of a psyche into new form.

1970
Altars

THE BAPTISM OF DESIRE

Starting in again, a glass of cold water I
toss at you beautiful hiding & laughing on my
part of the bed, you jumped into my bath I
sat on the toilet shaking with laughter while
you bathed & when my turn came
the water was lukewarm, as I shivered
in it only up to my crack you posed
& giggled—So I chase you through this poem, to
spurt cold at you again, dancing woman on
my part of the bed, figure now involved with
curtains I would hang for you to giggle &
twist over your naked stomach & breasts,
but we don't have curtains, the sunlight pours
daily in, open to green oleander & Japanese
gardener's abashment, how strange to love &
sleep before open window, embrace you & watch
human twigs or sweet stones half submerged
in mud, this house the regeneration of Japanese
house from which nature was outside, each
yellow butterbur pain, obsessed with nature
since there my nature was withheld, a glass
of cold to toss liquid flame in the energy that is
joy, hear the blue-headed birds hit pane they see
only a world opening, blue-feather smear over
king-sized bed our one possession here, light
that is tossed back & forth, tepid water I
gladly sit in adore you Queen Sheba-ing with
towel what a lovely embrace the light water body
on the one road with heart, what a simple
throne bed is to lie sleep & peek at you
O lovely rhythm that does not need myth other
than blue bird feather smear a pain coronation
head of the bed that my head can spill Protean
spermacetti without wincing since you are terminal
& again my train arrives

              Poem that drifts down to
the boy in tub she who is dead now bathed & can I
keep the glass of cold water tossing to you who
flirt in the folds of memory, figure of lovely Caryl
you are strong enough to let this dash of water be

potato & weenie, the knotty-pine dining-room with
porthole window where the boy filled with protein did
not know an Austrian doctor had made a last judgement
to affirm love life of 12 years old, & as the cold water
tosses it is wind at the end of Boulevard Place over
untying of newspapers to trundle on my route

                                This present beauty
I know of you not unlike my vision of her, vision I tossed
in again in Japan standing on the island mid Higashiyama-
road & watched the white linens toss on second story
roofs, there an innocent beholding of my mother the
photo of her at marriage lovely the photo of my father
at marriage lovely, I copulated them in the pain of
rooted to island waiting for the streetcar to carry me
downtown Kyoto 1963, seven years, but 28 years to
suddenly not in grass but in living memory sense
them, & the boy rushes in mind to put them in love
the white flapping towels & linen, All commingling of
light & clothes the desperate first, & I rushed cold
water into that possible image, no body to be hit but
road & rode downtown, & that was the pain to have no
terminal for first sprinklings of joy

                                & so she bathed the
crack of the boy insisted I not shower not linger in
bed at morning, those covers are still warm in the bed
over which life does seem to toss, a glass of cold
can be Arctic or can be joy & I love my first imaginings
of my mother tho no net caught the fish my mind/body
is, to throw & to throw in the throe that is the poem
your body Caryl the water dribbles down, runs to
foot of the bed that runs on its rails of world from
boy to man, there is a bed, one, we always inhabit
we are born in are nursed in fuck are lonely in &
sleep, this bed primally the door we open & close,
& you Caryl swirling flesh campanile sweet leaf
risen from the bloody waves,

                                This is no myth, it is
my life & the dogs that tear at the beautiful flesh in
Botticelli while the drinkers rear from their picnic
tables in alarm are watersparkle from your body
you walk on the water I throw & I live on the water you
breathe & my mother in sunlight a halo of energy I
will have here around you, I see Gladys Eshleman

through the halls of the golden string of imagination, I
see the thirty-five stages of my years of her life, she
is the curtains, the opaque folds we won't have in our
life, she is the backdrop my imagination loves to
see you dance against, playing at the organ & playing
pedaling the organ, pressing my feet down into deep
wood of boyhood piano scales upon scales dragon of
green Victory Stamps my little ass on the needlework
rose of piano-bench *Teaching Little Fingers To*
throw the glass, press down *Play* & learn to walk
index over third finger the endless bass somber through
The Rustle of Spring, Revolutionary Etude ultimately
Bud Powell who swirls in the curtain of the letter,
that black woman who crossed the hospital parking-lot
as she spoke her last coherent words to me the mind
wants to make Kali, black death goddess crossing
parking-lot having laid her cancer stinger of endless
hunger in the pitiful old woman wild & nut-colored on
the bed! All I know has rushed from me protein so
Proteus may live, if there must be shadow which is
myth I want it that close, not have to speak death in
black attendant heavy towards her car 7 stories down
from the monolithic wings of hospital, absence of angel
angel only in the glass you have poured full & I toss
& toss this cold water wake up my mother from the
last dreadful slumber by walking in unannounced

                    "oh, hello, Clayton . . ."
how much water is there in this glass, smell of pepper
tree, dried oleander flower, stand in California back
yard & know sex-economy is the energy household
sprinkle of Aquarian stars of the woman I am pouring
out, shallow pool on concrete, how much can she
pour who is pouring through me? No way to know other
than to not fear the pouring, curtainless window is
to pour & to pour & now I am upon you shielded
before the carnation bones of funeral lime-colored
Flanner & Buchannan the lavender-brocaded casket
with its heavy silver bars weight of weenies in my
plate weight of porthole window weight of the haunt
of house. I think my mother is consumed in this end-
less glass, treat decently this energy household this
is thy core of ecology to live in a body maybe to end
up nut, wild child, mother as man alone in the spinal
woods of monster losing her hair, sack-cloth of cancer to
ram food at one's mouth, smear into teethless gums

a morsel of bad-smelling fish, confuse coffee-cup with
pot & see her legs the accuracy of Grünewald's vision
of the Christ, mottled & damp in sores legs that in
hose were monument by piano my fingers pressed in
& in, that this IS a casket lowered into shovel-sliced
Menonite earth, that this is the end of man over which
rain & fog drizzle in the face of the sad Eshleman tribes,
pink rabbit-eyed faces of northern Indiana women huddled
in the unending death of no one ever throwing water on
the possibility of happiness, is not this the meaning of
rain, is not this the meaning of sunlight to not let
hideous rabbit, the wild child, park in the center of
our longing? Are not these jumpings on the mattress,
the dash to the faucet & run after you laughing
the meaning of life? And what monument more than to
gauge her drift through me, the satanic point at which I
would not turn on the tap but deny the spiritual economy
keep the glass empty, which, in the strength of her wish,
would have been not to write but play out the piano into
the settled negation that is Indianapolis. O mother, it
was in Kyoto I beheld thy triple-negation at the point I
first knew you were my mother! O tonight I would crown
that point, that you came to me there in the fury of
unacted desire & through a spider, abdomen red &
swollen, in the heat of summer transmitted to me
Isis, that who prunes us to let creation through seeks
likewise our scattered members, & the boy at 12
who stood by white pickets behind the garage while
Reich was actually thinking about him in Europe,
that boy a page before the court of women attacked
by mastiffs, who stood trembling while the white
table-cloths soaked in the wine, this boy before
the overturned banquet of humanity you brought to
bear upon the suffering spider body, who could through
such rabbit-eyed tradition manifest yourself, for
the fountain you had at least to plant—you left your
stacking of coins at least an instant to take on the
spider body & be again the beginning of world.

1970
Coils

THE BRIDGE AT THE MAYAN PASS

Five nights stone
has crowded in, to
say my father's
face is stone, to

dress his face in
the stone of
stone that speaks more
powerfully as

the father of my
father & his father
but I can only love
that which is no

more impersonal than
my seeing of
myself, & since I have
no childhood memory of

my father's face
I have been rocked to the edge
of Last Judgement, I
was moving toward

eternal fire, across the bridge
I was building of
the poem, had put on
that Mayan bridge

a hunched form, in the darkness over
the swaying pass, below us
the abyss I sought to
watch a huge wounded

shoulder of a form roll
into, Goya's Satan this Christ
I thought, & adored
the phantasmagoria of

Billy Graham in bra &
garters, like the Rhine-
gold girl, serving the
pitiful legions of Eshleman

beer, in the nave, the
elders who are
my Presbyters. But to bring
lightning here, to

smear a face, which
as A face is
His face, into stone, to
establish the gaping

cisterns of Tlaloc's eyes
as *my father's face,* my
marriage of
heaven & hell, evades

my feelings about the living
man. Tonight I remembered
a flicker, a wince
of suffering, very

quick, an instant, a
flicker stronger than stone
across the mortuary
lobby I saw, in

his face, as I turned from
the relatives who had
turned from him, & saw
him, suddenly

alone. He stood
on the bridge &
looked for me, I was
simply a wider

flicker, burning with more
hate & more love
than he, No—with no
more hate, no more

love than is here, this
bridge of ceaselessly
eroding alarm, this
bridge in a stronger

moment I call the
golden string. But the fiber of
the string is likewise creaking
wood & wind,

it holds the entire
phantasmagoria of the
weighted dread
I am & I am & I am.

II

But I refuse to contend
with *your stone*! I have been there, consciously, father, you
have not! You are in under her, the stone she lies on,
I fought with you in Vallejo, I struggled to
kill Vallejo at stone
my contention with man!
I am sick to death
of what won't stink!
Caryl is alive, Matthew
is alive, am I
alive? SICK TO DEATH
of baptism without desire,
& I know through the worm,
through the humility at odds
with woman is, the magic
of your unreadable runes!
You are the stone
a boy cannot read,
I write to make
to Matthew Matthew
visible, that a fucking
transmission be made!
But this stone ground, how
long will the Indian
patch up San Cristobal his huts,
skulls, his houses, black
window eyes, eyes, a thousand
black eyes candle-lit over our

Christ-leaden city of Lima!
My god, father, you didn't even know
we were in Lima! You voting
& voting & not even knowing
[lacunae]
[lacunae]
in the Indian's water supply, in
the copper lines that extend like
intestinal cords between here &
South America, STONE!
You didn't even know what you were doing when you fucked
      Gladys!
Her one erotic memory was a choir-master in Chicago who around
      1930 looked at her!
I am angry at you because you didn't know how to fuck!
I am angry at you because having moved through the superficial
      layers of her death I do not reach the living,
but hit you! I am furious at you because you don't know what goes
      on in Lima!
I hate you because when you traveled to Lima you couldn't look at a
      starving child but went to Macchu Picchu!
FOR THAT IS THE ADORATION OF STONE!
I HATE STONE, I bring pieces of it into my room only to weight
      the pages from the wind
on which the honest words of men who have lived through their
      lives live!
I HATE THE STONE IN MAN,
I HATE THE ADORATION
   OF YANG MARKS
   IN BUFFALO PAINTINGS
   & YIN CIRCLES BEFORE WHICH
   THE SITTING WORLD ADORES
   THE HISTORY OF MAN!
I hate you because you are simply a cruddy uninteresting piece of this
      history!
Because you would watch
   black children bring you a newspaper & not give them a Xmas tip
but would give white children a Xmas tip,
& because you would chase children away from the buckeye tree
      because they crept into the yard while I was 8 sitting back of the
      porthole window wishing I was creeping into our yard to steal the
      unquestionably free fallen buckeyes!
And so you are in me, & I feel my hate for you my mother dies!
My mother dies! Yes, complex knot of real feeling through which
      burning rivulets leaked, her tears awakened my going-to-
      hell cheeks, & you sitting 30 years in the slaughter house

creeping, your pen, across the ledger, coming home with your
bloodstained coat tips, that I had only those rainblooddrops to
imagine what you were drawing salary from! The nerve of you,
to not break down ever once & WEEP with the blood of a steer
on the heels of your Charlie McCarthy shoes! The nerve of you
not to cry! The nerve of you never to blast me! The nerve O the
NERVE dead, dead & dead & dead & dead *dna dead dna DEAD*
Yoru roars! Yes, the faculty that otherwise is literary careful
sadness, literary adolescence forever wrapped in the many-colored
coat of myth, what a Joseph coat you are, Ira Clayton Eshleman,
& all the neighbors all picking around in the suburbs looking with
flashlights for the murderer of a girl, you do not come home father,
I will not let you come home, for home is where you'd like to flicker
    forever, flicker a wince or a sad distressed look, lacunae
lacunae, sad distressed look lacunae, lacunae honorably in Catullus
Villon, lacunae in the parts of man
uttered & lost in paper-rot, but damn lacunae of what is never
    uttered!
AND I WILL NOT LET YOU REMAIN STONE
FOR STONE IS
ANCIENT FIRE
I HONOR ANCIENT FIRE
FOR TOTALLY NON-CHRISTIAN REASONS
I WOULD NOT CONSIGN YOU TO ETERNAL FIRE
The ancient fire! The ancient fire! Old fire! Anger & blessing, hate
desire, concern, sympathy, intermingling, Yes, this is
under Last Judgement, old pisco taste of last judgement,
music, song be DAMNED, the raw voices on benches at 12,000 feet
    be
held, the ancient men are those who have no clothes! Those men be
let in, those unlit roadways, those failures of rain
YES I AM A BABY INCAN
I RUN THE FULL CIRCLE OF THE YANG MARKS
I SEE THE ONLY THING WORTH ADORING IS MY ART
IN WHICH THOSE I LOVE ARE NOT ABSENT
And the lure of forgiveness is
consumed in the meaning of understanding
THE MEANING OF STONE IS
IT BE FUCKED ON OVER A BED OF
DOWN EVERY SECOND DAY IN THE LIFE OF MAN
And the yang marks will be seen a movement
And the yin will be seen as movement
For the meaning of movement is the body of man & woman & child
Against rock to love & keep warm
THIS IS HISTORICAL UNDERSTANDING
And the generations of Eshleman, oh let them huddle, yes, with wine

66

& candles on a rope bridge over a Mayan Pass! Yes over the abyss,
the whole white spook-show like Witch Sabbath! Great black
    shadows,
let them pass the wine, unhuddle, let my father be among his people,
Let there be that picnic with the abyss beneath, let spastic Dean
Eshleman touch Matthew that Matthew not be confused, I open this
    cyst
that Matthew wander fully among these generations, let him see Iva
Eshleman's madness, THIS IS THE WEIGHT, Charles, Sylvia,
    Orville,
Leonard, Helen, Almira, Ira, Olive, Aunt Barbara never seen from
    Florida,
(these are the "books"), Fern, Faye, Bob Wilmore (these in Blake's
age *Generations of Man*), THE WEIGHT THE DREADED
    WEIGHT I

NOW TAKE OFF INDIANA

I RELEASE INDIANA

NAILED MILE GALED IN ANSWER

TRACED IN HEIL THY NATURN FACE!

1970
Coils

II
SCORPION HOPSCOTCH

THE PHYSICAL TRAVELER

I woke up pregnant by a wall
where a red spider watched me
from its web; don't forget, it
told me as I rose, that I

am pregnant too but dependent
on my web. A mobile pregnant
man I walked along the wall
& as I walked the wall began to

talk, I don't want you anymore that
now you're full of me, get
lost. But you're the father of my
state I tried to hold

it from going, but it was wide &
I was small, so wide I saw
it ran around Creation
which seemed a city

within, & I pregnant with
a little wall without. What would
you do in my place?
I began to bore

into the father of my state
but as I drilled & drilled
I found my benefactor
was deep proportionate to

my drill, while on each side of
the passageway I was making
Creation seemed to abound
When I turned to retreat

I found a woman in my way
She sat crouched in my passage
head tucked between her
knees, I tried to push her out

I tried to see her face
I couldn't budge her from the shaft
& so I joined her to
my fate by pushing her up

inside me through my recent
gate. Now under double charge
I attacked the father of my
plight, the wall gave way

I stood in Creation the air
like yolk each form like running
blood I gave way like my wall
& loosed my nature

through my thighs a woman &
a little wall attached like Siamese
twins, I could get rid of them
but she could not be

free of it. You're the father of
my yoke she cried & then
I saw her face, in Creation
each things weds &

counterweds, no one steps on
someone's spine, I lost them here
Her face boiled orange
with fire & empty

I started to shred into the flow
but I remembered the spider's
words & so strove out
of Paradise, maintained

my womblike form. And now,
because of this, I appear
to be a man & while the spider
stays my kin

I can no longer hear its voice
except when I press my ear to
any wall & all my emptiness
shakes with awe

for I remember my father
I remember the night
he crept into my cell
& my crib ran red.

1972
Coils

STUDY FOR A SELF-PORTRAIT AT 12 YEARS OLD

In his grandfather's toilet
the enjoyment of porcelain, varnished wood,
mingled pipes' bulges, twisting
his new power, apprehension, where
did it swirled away go, dark lucent
days that lightning
prickled, for *they*
were outside the door he hesitated to
lock, they'd hear the latch, they were
the lightning and
its cartoon, the cracks
in his childhood he was leaving? He didn't
know, he drifted
in night's humid tent, only
at grandpa's did he sleep *by* them and now
they seemed so huge and near by,
their silence, their unmoving . . .
what *did* he want? He'd play
now under their bed in the afternoon
excitedly putting soldiers between the springs,
cleaning the dust off and liking the tightness of
his body under a great friendly bed,
how he wanted to join them
to know where it swirled away to.
Under the bed he realized he could
hide there until they got in bed—
he would be missed—so he'd have to leave
that thing leaving him on his cot
to deceive them, so *he* could know—
it was then he divided
fully, compared to this
the fun on the toilet always had an end,
but this leaving them his body so *he*
could know, *this* was conception!
So he stayed there, under the bed
when they said good night to him on
his cot—heard them lie down—
their silence—their unmoving? or the density
between him and them? Couldn't tell,
and couldn't go back to Charlie
McCarthy tucked in on the cot, so he began to climb,

insinuating himself between the springs
and once up through them, locked
between their funnel tops and the mattress,
he *had* to go on—he bit
into the tufted cover, gnawed a hole
big enough to draw his head and shoulders
into, losing all *sense* of them now,
for once into it they seemed the other
side of the world! But he could
still remember, he knew they were near,
breathing on and away from the matter
that all his body had entered—his
body? Seemed to be lessening, he was
more and more his act, gnaw and tunnel
gnaw and tunnel, then direction
likewise went, *was* he moving up or
horizontally under them? Sometimes
the stuffing had a taste, of body sludge or
bits of skin, he tried to judge, was it
theirs? Or his grandparents' or people
like he'd seen in pictures of caves?
Impossible to know, the fear if he stopped
gnawing was awful so he kept on
pulling along with his loom-motion,
new born but mountainously lost
in what, when thought, appeared conception
but, in movement, was burial, within which
he was to go on and on.

1974
The Gull Wall

CREATION

I raise for you
become light, weighted,
I thrill from what I
sense as center, released

and bound, airy,
even as meat I am power,
but contingent upon you
enclosing me, some of me, enough

to stir the twin sleeping
to kick, cry, scream
as I go down in you gravity
for a moment rejects me,

for a moment gravity
is ejection, out
of you I swarm not as an ego
but an example of man,

in that moment the matter
yielded to is overcome,
I feel its heat
beyond the shield of my own

bifurcation, my thought-seeds
give up becoming children,
so mutually do we exchange
this happens, I abandon

my deadness, my twin
abandons its wall, art
flies into place,
I become spacial,

gratified enough to love
imagination, to go from our bed
to the trapdoor
and peer out into what

for a spider is wired meadow
I am furred, my face
resembles a bucket — or
is it a pillow, buried

happy by your shoulder,
under a fly's blue
screens black truffle meat
glistens, a slender figure

the Venus of Lespuge rises
buried in gross
maternal body, until you spread
the place of parental stone

I gnaw and tunnel,
feeling your living pressure in
their bodies' dents
I raise

through you into
that Venus,
leaving my buttocks
as a fly's eyes,

the earth is foetal
swimming, with flippers,
face upward, lonely
I want to enter its anthill,

the moment I envision it
feminine, it displays its masculinity,
a 20 foot clay nest bars
my entry.

1974
The Gull Wall

SUGAR

With her hair set by her mother with water & sugar
what sweetness the bees tasted intoxicated by the little blonde
lost in high grass a few yards from the house
But what does a mother know about sweetness
A mother like hers could only dream of Shirley Temple
handing candy after candy so her little girl would love her
This is why Caryl Reiter loved sour pickles
My heart is aroused thinking of her solitary walk once each week
to the pickle store where she would taste a pickle still fresh
yet briny & sweet come dripping from the barrel one nickle &
savor it all the way home isolate childhood savoring its pickle
against the sweetness that is granulated & false
When Caryl Reiter was 12 she was an hour late home one night
her father locked her out she wandered to the corner & found a
    policeman
& told him My father locked me out Will you help me get in?
She remembers her father kicked her down the hall after
I have no experience like this in my childhood
I drowsed years that Caryl Reiter was fighting
my little energies dreamed & strengthened while I
obeyed my hair cut & combed like my father's
a little Charlie McCarthy a little wooden boy
with his heart dreaming & nourishing enormous spores
which would suddenly march forth 20 years later
virginal & green but with that peculiar hound-crashing-out-of-hell
    timing
by which a few leave the midwest
& thus Caryl Reiter struggles for energy today to live
So much given to the blind & greedy parents
who drink & drink pouring each week more honey into
the blonde well that erupts its fierce innocent angers
but loses like the frog that jumps up one step but falls back two each
    day

     *

A wink
from mother,
a big wink,

78

almost an elbow nudge
that she was getting an extra bag of sugar
Dilbert's Grocery Bensonhurst 1946
rationed days, an extra bag of sugar *free,*
Caryl Reiter at her mother's side wondering
flirt? what is she doing, with this man? who is not,
my father? I am 4
& walked out into the world is unreal
Things are not what they
& cried hysterically while her mother tugged her home
I watch Caryl Reiter's mother the wink
still on her rouged cheek pulling
What rot in that wink, or
what sweetness I should say,
a kiss on the grocer's cheek
so Caryl Reiter could be attacked by bees
A pretty little girl
so her mother could dream I am a good mother
the grocery-man's cock delicious & smelling of flowers
just for a wink pulling
Caryl Reiter down the street The weight of hysteria fled
22 years later I smoked a joint one afternoon & when I
got up from the bed my arms got up too, my body was lifting &
    light
I was back on that street, back in Dilbert's a wink traveling 22 years
suddenly pops The world is unreal
4 year old Caryl Reiter I am in love with you
I am rushing from the store having hidden behind the counter
You are right I cry,
I am a beautiful soft-eyed man who does not want your mother's
    kiss,
a soft llama-eyed man, my mellow pupils tinged rose & azure,
a llama pretending to be a man
who stops before you for you to admire & stroke,
you can stroke my neck my back you can kiss my pretty ear
I am the confirmation of your 4 year old vision,
the confirmation to return to you, a fulness to plug
the gap you've just opened The world *is* unreal
You may kiss my furry belly
Fondle my amazing tail

  *

The strawberries have been covered with sugar for the hundredth
     time
Caryl Reiter has finally thrown them at her mother
"I don't WANT any sugar on MY strawberries!"
"*I* didn't put any there!"
or as when Caryl Reiter's father constructed a safe to keep
his coins in her mother bored through the bottom so that each
carefully deposited coin fell into her greedy hole
Now it is the moment Caryl Reiter's father has come to collect
his savings, to feel the weight of his coin horde
Lo it is empty, not one fifty cent piece
Who could have bored through the bottom?
"ME? I didn't do it"   sugar like steel
A wall of sugar
filled with safe holes
Now Caryl Reiter's mother has found a cigarette hole in her blouse
She is ironing & thinking of the grocer's blind & loving cock
Furiously she is ironing & thinking of Caryl Reiter
riding a stallion in impertinent triumph before her ironing eyes
but she is so full of sugar all direct accusation is frozen in her tongue
"I know you are smoking" insisted again & again, 3 days of hysteria
"and someone told me they saw you in the cemetery *with some boys*"
Caryl Reiter has grown wise she is pondering what *is* her mother
thinking yes I was in the cemetery with the boys but didn't do
     anything wrong
So what? And the ironing mother in the heat of her feel for
     tombstones
before inwardly hurt but smiling, kind of grinning kind of laughing
Caryl Reiter with a dog-collar ankle bracelet
Caryl Reiter in slingback black shoes
Caryl Reiter grown beyond pinafores in a stretchtop with a topless
     brassiere
nylons on Sunday because her Catholic friend wore them,
in leopard pants, lipstick painted over her lips,
Caryl Reiter winking at her mother
Caryl Reiter who is the friend of Gooik who used to hit & bite her
Caryl Reiter whose childhood I am in love with

Now I may return to Clayton's bedside
& smile at his cataracted eyes wet with dying,
the tie they wrapped around his neck
& put a suit on him even though he lays in bed wet
with his stubbled chin his finger through the wetness of his eyes
smiling and going kitchikitchicoo tickling my shirt button
the ghost of kitchikitchicoo like a flame under the broth of
the childhood of Caryl Reiter

For the truth of it is I was the grocer
sweating in my uniform each day for the sight of Irene Reiter
desiring to give her a free bag of sugar & much more
& even touched by the little sweetheart at her side.

1973
The Gull Wall

from ADHESIVE LOVE

Embracing, fervently embracing, in the embrace itself the bud of imagination is born, as if one was asleep before, suddenly as excitement mounts mind is stimulated, yet this stimulation is felt moving toward orgasm as a part of the physical excitement itself,
    it is the creation of the world,
    the closed triptych of *The Garden of Earthly Delights,* the earth swaddled in fog, the light-blue uroboric fog,
    orgasm opens the triptych to.
    It opens to—
orgasm is not interior painted surface, but only orgasm will rain down on that little bud trembling up to mind, trembling up through the entire body in the fervency of embrace, and after the triptych opens, after I lose control of myself in you, cry out and throb, discharging the phantom of myself, the triptych is open, I lie back, softly head against your breast, my eyes closed I dream into it, the orgasm so intense that I dream awake, often I see a green glade, figures moving about, fields, bright blue skies,
    or if my eyes are open
    what would otherwise be visual is words, sometimes words from nowhere, words I have never thought, formations, gratitudes, or words I have thought, phrases, near-poems, infused, covered with a wonderful gauze, I smell your sweet breasts, doze, forgetting and remembering.
    But of course when I arise I begin again—I could say the poetry was in those moments of blissful reverie, that what is written down is tragic because it is always in some way an attempt to recover the very instant of inspiration when the image or formation is most bud-like there,—and that is true for the individual soul. For the individual soul the magnificence is in that rain of embrace contacting the little bud of mind reaching up wanting O wanting to be touched—it is that touch that tells a man or a woman I AM—tells them *There is something more here than this pleasurable or aching biology. What I call my body or my biology is but a fleck of what I am—*
    And that reassurance must be given in the bone,
    cannot come just as idea, as another's experience—
and when it does come we have a great proud experience, we feel ten feet tall and we fit nowhere, and then we awake into another consciousness that that ten foot arrogance, that great proud dwelling, is just that—is our individual soul, and if we live by it, if we try to live by it we are as Gulliver in a world of little people—and to have the soul *And* to see beyond the having of it, to have it and to see most other people for the little people they are—this is the beginning of compassion—it is unbearable, and the budded soul is trapped by the very consequence of *perception outside of itself*—for if it stays within itself, knows it is soul, wetted in fervent

82

embrace and remains there, it becomes moldy and eventually rots; for to be wet is to grow, and the growth is out of the bed, man woman like vine, or any combination of lovers, a great double vine loaded with the vegetation of knowledge slowly climbing, great muscled creeper, green and demanding, out of spore, out and out, until the original pulsation achieves itself, flowers.

So the writing down, the making of art at large, is not really tragic once one sees that the act is accountable to *more than the individual soul.* For from the viewpoint of my desk the imaginative bud given in embrace turns into fantasy; that is, I am here now, with all my desire, in spite of everything, to say I am—*without* you. If you and I, Caryl, are gratified, if the love is genuine, then I do not long back to the bed from the desk— but if the bud did not unite there, O what a misery it is to be here! What an awful re-vision, what a remaking and remaking, that collapsed image of creation as masturbation, the poor self-denying soul praying, in effect, God at least let me get it off here in my head! And it is out of such denial in the place of biological spore that most of what we recognize as wit or cleverness, "literature" in contrast to poetry, comes. The "academic," the "formula poem," that which feeds off other artists' genuine experience, all that sad rippling extension of the genuine stone plunked into the pool— but not the stone's own ripples—no, more as if occasionally a stone were to be plunked in and go straight about its business to the bottom, and these ripples were waiting over there in the pond grass and came out gently sucking at the stone's centrific power.

1973
The Gull Wall

TRIPTYCH

Left Panel: Portrait of Vincent van Gogh

I will hold my hand in this fire
to speak to her, I will stay in
the fire of this world long enough to
speak to her, I will place myself in
the hands of my own Covering Cherub to
speak to her, for I am not seeking to
marry her, but to speak to her,
deep in a mine, in the wall
I drill through, my speech to her is
my art, I can
be bent, I can double back, I can as
the beggar be bent backward heel to nape
in sleep, in the mine as they chip at her,
strike dead speak from her, dead spirals.
In the night the stars hang out in sinister places
they put their heads together, I take Death to
where their heads are together, where the mother is
lost in His washing her free, Her I must speak to,
for she is my Covering Cherub, my wall &
my boring through, my wall &
almond-tree branch, I will hold to
this fire for 10 years, my hand in her
a Biblical motion, churned
chair, churning candle on churning chair,
chair churning sky, in my room, in
what is dear, I place a candle on this bottom,
in the basement of maternal hold, I place it to blaze
cock up, where the stars hang out
sinister armchair, where the stars cock & claw,
where the claims churn, where my name
manure, my name Vincent is shared
peasant, mine, her ass hiked — but
the desire to split it open is
to split open the extent of the known world!
I have been where others claim to have seen,
I have been olives built Jerusalem-blue mountains
poured back my love into this rec-writhe, this rec
tangular, this bone lay-mansion, I smolder
in the Rembrandt mansion of, where the fire I am in is

rouge, There is continuity, and there is this broken
rectangle, broken triangle, broken
single line—I will hold my hand in this fire
I will speak to her as I know the world is but a glimpse
of the wall of my tunnel, almond-tree branch for the baby,
but life, life itself! for me! Hiked ass prehistoric
entrance, I do not answer the door because I
know Artaud knocks, I want to go into that ass
and paint, I want to use her organs and paint her
insides, to take her organs and use her blood to paint
her goosepimply coils, almond-tree branch for the baby,
almond-tree branch for me, rose, hollyhocks, zinnias, peonies,
pansies, carnations, cineraria, delphinium, aster,
lilacs, daisies, anemones, I came out of her cunt
I want to return through her ass, my Covering Cherub
pecks about in the yard, the chicken I am
bothers around with nothing, I can only paint
8 or 9 hours a day, the thrust I make is my Covering,
Winged Seed, my own angelic ghost, my seed
haunting my desire O my people, all people to paint
for you! To literally remake the world into a universe of
lilacs, daisies, cineraria, aster I came out of your cunt
I want to return through your stem, what is dead in
me is my Covering Cherub, This is why I paint
aster, aster why do you cover me? Why am I trapped
in the visual box of you and me? That you are the bottom of
and I am the side, Being, trapped, cornered
in thought, and all those needies outside—
but her, her—why have I damned my life giving
woman's soul to almond-tree branch, why have I sought
her, why sought to speak only to her, Only
that the buttock church, this rest from the storm, was
stalagmited with the iron that breaks through in spring
through the earth, this iron my body needs
aster, phylox, this hollyhock, I needed to eat her ass
and my anguished famished jaws only
painted what unrolls in the lagoon.

1973
The Gull Wall

Central Panel: Frida Kahlo's Release

Where I came from
is the accident's business . . .

exactly, how it made
thirty-five bone grafts
out of my impaled investment.
My dear father is here, not
off photographing monuments,
which he did so well,
in spite of epilepsy,
he took some
of the terror when the streetcar
created me. How those of us,
determined by one thing,
come forth
is no less complex
than you who are multifoliate.

My face unpacks
the corner of Cautemozin and Tlalpan highway,
"a simple bonze
worshipping the Eternal Buddha,"
van Gogh's words, that other
dear epileptic, whom I took to bed
in honor of my father,
I let both repose me—
I lead with my right cheek
thus profiling my left.
For a moment I was seated
straight up in Vincent's chair,
and because the light behind me and
my body were infested
with incombustible sulphur,
I am sister to a double putrefaction.

We who are singly determined
we too dream toward paradise
even though our outpour is contractive,
"one dimensional," you say,
"she only paints one thing,"
you, do you paint anything? And if
you do, is your ease
hard enough to skate? And if it is,

do the figure eights of your admirers ever
come to more than arabesqued return?

My face is rubbed
back into the shaft of human
bluntness. Its point
is to tamp seed
into eroded furrows of pain,
to look back at this life to say
exactly what the soul looks like,
exactly what life looks like,
exactly, what death!
Worn Coatlicue rememberings,
scabbed twistings in the flannel of rock,
I was so handled,
such a sugared skull,
I lived through carnivals
of my own organs, a cornucopia of processed fowl.

The others were off rutting in a firework haze.
I was lobstered in my chair shell,
balancing my vision on the spinal
crockery strewn about me,
shards of an exhumed prayer.

I drew paradise up close about my shoulders,
I gave monkeys my shoulders as well as my breasts,
I let them look through your eyes to Brueghel
where Flemish scapes fade back to Job
under a spreading oak, the Adamic Job,
amphibious, caressing his progeny
(As Diego lowered, segment by segment
upon me, khaki and emerald
Behemoth mottlings dressed my injury).

I know the dry riverbed of illness
where orgasm's rachitic child
crawls in place. Gamy iodine on a silver plate,
I transformed the hospital linen
into more than a daguerreotype of paradise.

Pray no more for me, Mother of Unending Lightning—
illuminate the bleeding pulqueria nips
where gaiety, slaughter-equidistant,
shishkabobs the sun
through a cellular catacomb of moons in

the quilted night sky pulsing
with El Greco bellows. Under the Mass
are the vast lamb wafers in the Mexican kiln
slid in at 4 a.m. on Christ-crusted rays.

I am fused to the inability to
reproduce what does determine me
with its unborn baby hand
which I finally learned to wear as earring in
the Galapagos Trench pressure
outside within what our species has lived.

1978
What She Means

Right Panel: Portrait of Francis Bacon

I will both
hold my hand in that fire
and not, the fire
of pigment where character

is an act of the brush.
Vincent how
innocently you sighted what
I see, a buxom

assed woman
vibrating with the earth
vibrating before a church,
Why is it there?

There for praise
it tells you, and you
who have felt desire know where
that heat is kept,

its safe, where what you
will not give is stored,
where you pull
back so the come

smarts and rears back
up into the anus,
pullback, Satan,
smarting anvil

where the pullback is
hammered into Sunday
goers, anal pouches
filled

the Buttock Church is
congregated, pews
stacked with non-human
beings who face in

hymn back to the back-
turned altar
behind which Pan
is a semen gleaming

the moment before it
hits that redhot anvil.
I see my model
seated crosslegged on

that bone between
anus and sex,
he has for his aura
the enormous

fire of Pan, King
Kong sized
but only the shadow,
inside the shadow

a man
on a bicycle
collapsing,
wobbling three

ways at once,
inside his head
Mauthausen
mound of eyeglasses,

an attendant scoops
a shovelful, it's
garbage, into George
Dyer's lower body,

my model
slips his aura
like a rotten snood,
leaves his platform

and walks over to
where I sit, hooked
on my own emission,
a man in tension,

ready to artificialize
everything.
We connect
against a canvas

stretched against
a concrete wall.
Rabid connection
in which I am penetrated

twisted on my own
cable, bled
and kissed,
in ecstasy and

bored, all at once.
Unable to burst
fully, the fight becomes
can I contain

a surreal grotesque,
can I make it stick
against the wind-
tunnel of our great

abstract age?
I know that bone
cave where Ulysses
lies face down in body

sludge, his arm
around his drunken
comrade Elpenor,
I have felt them crawled

by diamond-backed
maggots, and I have heard
the hags laugh
who crouch

about them, senile
and pregnant,
the *grotesca* who link
Rabelais Goya and Artaud.

I will hold my hand in that
fire as well as
another, I will watch
the other turn it, beyond

membrane, into a very
dear figure, the two burned
wings of impotence
and sensuality,

crunched in erection
a Swahili rises
from a European
chair, in the lavender

hood of his shaved
head he starts to cross
with a Mohawk
"they eat animate objects"

is fed into a white
computer at the far
corner of the same
world — Pan is not

dead his little hooves
kick out Krazy
Kat, Bumstead,
a Cubistic scimitar

in the guts
is part of my torsion.

I sow
my nerves

on the photographic
corpse of George
Dyer, what sprouts
I set inside what were

my heart and
life lines, a flimsy
seppuku cage
from which our semen

like the Banners of
Heartlessness flies.
I watch the antagonistic
combustion, it

pulls at my creation like
taffy, which cooks
now on its own power.
George-sprouting-Francis.

Yet the force of
abstraction
would finally suck
it into a stripe,

I must anchor my deposit
against a magenta
wall — I fit in Germanic
halos which

leech my Frankenstein
but hold it
in place:
between the wall's

dilating hole and
Vincent's old flame, his cock
snarled rubberbands around
the femurs of my patient.

1975
The Gull Wall

92

A VISIT FROM PAUL BLACKBURN

It is white blood I need,
can you bring it to me?
And I need to be shaved;
have you a barber's bowl
into which my let blood might fall?
White blood,
the next time you visit me,
it is small here,
too confined,
Can you bring me a razor?
Can you shave the blood
and the workmen pruning living matter
who make a terrible noise,
What drips down to me
through clay
is without nourishment,
through you Clay,
your picture of this place
is without nourishment
What drips down to me through
you Clay is nourishment,
her stain
her cucurbit! juice on a leaf
What drips down through clay
is nourishment
the Elixir on a leaf
say   say   say
I know what I want
Can you plant in her grain?
Can you place a cyclone in her throat
and pour in grain to swell her?
Can you stuff her with vibrations?
Can you work her into a lather?
Can you then catch her drippings on a leaf?
Can you churn nature
into foie gras to feed me?
For the dead taste
is in what she gives to
the rain settling

1974
The Gull Wall

THE SANDSTONE GATE

for Hayden Carruth

This happened long ago.
He had begun to see himself
instead of what his father saw
or so he thought.
He itched and stank, misunderstanding
the nature of what he was
he brought Maureen his rattles
and his books, thinking if I can just
get in all my troubles will be over.
Maureen said: "You may see me before and
after I see the one I entertain with my
Irish breasts" as she would smile
at what he was, they would read together
by her sandstone gate,
he thought: if I could just stretch myself into a size
to fit that gate
there'd be a warm bath inside
where I might rest
and draw signs of her
on the tub walls forever;
wrenching his mouth apart
got from his chest some cry:
a green cloud prickly and strong with
his stink, this he carried like a crown to her place
and while she was dallying with her suitor
he squeezed it into her milkbox—
yuk, what a poem, she tried to get it off her hands
how vile, and said nothing
for she kind of liked that
half of him looked like an old man
and half mirrored her, she liked
to fantasize two people
making love to her, she dreamed of
her self as another her,
her her's sex grasped her head
while her sex grasped her father's head,
for hours she would lie in the tub
stoned on what seemed the ultimate equilibrium;
meanwhile the one who thought
he had begun to see himself

was like a mouse in her wall,
a tendril she knew sooner or later would poke through.
She considered: he is ceasing to be a dope,
only so much longer can I read with him on the floor
then introduce him for the nth time to my suitor,
or call him late at night when my suitor has left
and invite him to sit with me on the floor until dawn
soulfully missing each instant the point of life—
she knew he wanted in
and that if she let him in he might
not withdraw but go on into her tub
install himself there for good;
well, she found a way, she parted
the silk curtains which appeared to
hang before a window but which actually
covered her great sandstone gate;
with all her might she pressed and pressed
contracting the gate to diaphragm size
and slipped it into her sex where it miraculously
grew phalanges and anchored itself convex
to the outside; he was knocking and she let him in
letting him this time after 10 minutes unhook
her brassiere, a flimsy thing it glowed hieroglyphic
a doily of radium to his eyes crossed in inner itch,
she felt herself picked up and carried to
within inches of what he thought the gate,
she heard him hit, bluebird against her window
then a distant pounding, some neighbor working
on his fender with a rubber hammer . . .

       Crazed he stumbled
out into what was no longer Bloomington
but the ruins of an ancient Hindu city,
he was looking for some salve, something to ease
that ache, the absurdity of looking for ointment in
a rubbled field, but he was still caught up
perhaps more now than ever in his father's
values, everything was dust, he was
fixed about an idea, bent over it, his legs
wrapped around an enormous sandstone gate or goddess
which jerked and bumped around the ruins,
o mother he thought if only
you'd get me off this! presto, there she was, or
as much of her as he might reasonably expect,
a young woman wearing a mask of her
looked up at him and beckoned him into her pit.

He stiffened, the goddess relaxed,
he fell then into a sleep of sensory
deprivation, shapes but no particulars,
he was in the tub but the goddess
had dressed him in rubber so while he floated
he could not feel, or had he ever really felt?
That became his strait-jacket
and he dreamed of Midas, to touch something
into gold since everything *appeared*
to touch him but did not; there were now two
outsides, that far filmy place called nature
and a closer outside, a one-inch void about him
which far nature seemed filtered through,
author sounds, or radio static,
he dreamed himself to the point Maureen in milk-
colored floorlength silk was advancing toward him,
benevolent, her arms outstretched,
he weighed tons crosslegged on the floor
in her corner, since she never reached him,
since he could not rise, his genital city
grew enormous; from his ruling tower
he decreed there were to be two castes of women,
the Emanation and
the Will—the first stayed so close to man, was so
warm and wavy, this caste was allowed to serve,
was treated with compassion and when elderly
retired to The Palace of the Doves;
the other had severed herself, no longer could
he feel her as something waving out of him,
independent she had power to potentially
oppose him—*oppose* him! He contemplated
The Palace of Entrails in which this caste
would be Iron Maidened.

1975
What She Means

A leaf, a weightlessness, a brother who never was, a little companion
    who never was,
fence post before Clayton, companion only of Jr.,
invisible for 40 years now simply a lost leaf, one of thousands in the
    driveway,
a Piglet, a natal daemon standing with snow cap pulled down so I
    cannot see his face,
I cannot tell if he is smiling under, or if his face is chewed up into
    an expression of fury,
fist-face, battered vegetable face, with a stone behind it or a present?
    Where did you come from?
Who sent you to my house? Surely you must be like me for I cannot
    play with anyone different than me,
surely you must have been sent by my mother, and if so,
must be my brother, for my mother would not send someone she
    herself did not have . . .
I must go out to you since it is so silent in my room and so
    beautifully silent in the deep snow
where you stand, herm, boundary marker between her and me,
    chum, faceless one,
do you love me? She must have known I was lonely, surely that is
    why she sent you, or
planted you in the snow, she must have felt me become a singular
    foetus in her, of all the goldenrod my father sowed
she must have felt you and thousands like you drown in the dust of
    her organs and leave her, an only mother with child . . .
So long have I tried to blind you out of my consternation not know-
    ing what you
were going to do to me, surely you must have seen me emerging
with my face from which a blowtorch was flaming, was that
why you pummeled me in the snow? But we could not have emerged
    hand in hand,
I was to be single, with you tacked to my chest,
planted so close you are involved with my most intimate laughter.

1976
What She Means

THE DRAGON RAT TAIL

for Norm Weinstein

Where my hope, naive
and controlled by a rote-ness
thought art might be
a single Japanese flower
deft in a bowl, my hope
to escape profusion,
a single flower, a red gleam,
one thing alone against
clay and wood—
　a poem began to grow
in the very room with
that wilting flower,
but it was an atmosphere of
a poem *can* be,
a poem is around here,
I took hold
between my crosslegged
legs of a string of rain,
it was to find something to pull
out, to put
into my mouth
an ancient story,
to find where
my tale began and pull
up, too physical
I knew, so physical
I would have to digest
the having of
a cock, gnaw
the archetype through,
the body
was good
but was attached
to an image I
could only sense, a rat
growing in the tatami,
I pulled
on a growing widening tail,
a contruction worker
pulling an endless alligator out of a sewer,

but through the tatami itself,
hideously embarrassed by
the closeness of the thing,
whatever it was, to my
own organs, that I was pulling
myself inside out, that the poem
I sought was my own menstrual
lining, as if suddenly one day
I would have my inside
out on the tatami before me,
a kind of flayedness, a cape,
something in words, but words
hooked together an anguish or
covering, a quilt, as if
Indianapolis had been pulled off
and the rawness remained,
flickering off and on off my nerves,
jagged aura, some of it grey
some of it blue, and under?
The rigidity pit
where Clayton and Gladys sweetly
wandered, looking up
in intense innocent
complicity with an image
I moved into, then out, then into in
their eyes; that is when Kelly cried
"Find them in the grass!"
he meant find the mothering
fathering powers which are not
your mother, father, find
and connect to what they are
the ghosts of—
I glimpse the Doppelgänger
they as well as I
were involved with,
personal and cultural
shadow in diamond light
striding across a stage.
      The scales increased—
a long green thing was
piano practice, apprenticework
took 16 years, diurnal,
inside the day the impossible
spine of saying all
that the day was
blocked me, I bent,

spine, over keys,
inside the machine a Christmas tree
glowed, and under it
puberty subincision,
I posed, by my dog, he
went off into the night,
I tried to reach a Japanese bar hostess
through my morality play,
my father pressed the flash-bulb,
Rilke fell out, compassionate,
distant, paper . . .
Rote screw-hive
alive but compressed into "God."
Days of sitting on the bench
and trying to bank a word
free from the roar of never
that quietly gnawed, given
my hold to the tail
which had not grown,
which had grown enormous—
"the moment of desire" Blake calls
it, break the judge
in highchair, bring that Jack Horner
that "Good boy" satisfied with
his plum dipped thumb into
the savage truth of this world:
people want love
only as a passive given,
they hate and actively
oppose love as an active opposition.
In Kyoto, faced with my dragon
rat tail I understood that the world
is adamant, that there is no way through it.
Gates, philosophies, arts, all "ways"
confronted orange mud running down
a twilit road on Sunday afternoon.
One way to get anything out: haul up
and sieve, engage the haul,
make the rat tail big, dragon tail,
make the dragon tail bigger than Jung,
bigger than all ideas,
let it engorge the house,
split the tatami! Ride
it! Not the moon, not
the nostalgia for that other place,
but the funk that struck inside

on the way home from the public bath.
Not to remember or realize the bath.
Be in the bath. Deal
with this other thing, art does not have to
lip the natural, live the natural,
jack off on her fender if I have to but
live the natural and confront
this other thing, sieve out
the little performer,
break the piano bench I was to become
an alcoholic upon, "Blue Moon"
"White Christmas" a chain of command,
break the chain, open it up and discover
the seed-chum she and he and all of them,
the whole atavistic octopus,
pumped into my wine cup, be
paranoiac, splay out, feel spiderlike
throughout the realm that paranoia
seeks to feel, understand the rigidity
pit is armor, something
I can get rid of,
yet it is bone, what
I stand in,
armorless armor,
my marrow, my
very scent, is
social, where I do not have to be,
where I am forever, as long as I
am alive, packed in with
who I am born to, alone, or
brothered, essentially with the ghosts of
the fathering mothering powers I
can transform to aid me.
My mother's dead eyes float out
bald in raving love for me,
how she knew what she wanted me to be
so confused was she in what I should be,
under the Betty Grable butt allowed on my closet door,
under the ghost games under the bed Saturday afternoon,
under my being allowed
to dress up in her girdle and twirl
the family safe, was *Liberace,* the person
she hoped I would be, fully middleclass,
artistic, gay, fully in command, a hero
wrapped in a 146
pound floor length black

mink cape lined with Austrian rhinestones,
a ghastly Virgil!

     Confidence
I pray, at 40, to lead this Doppelgänger out to pasture,
he cannot be done with,
I can only let him graze,
I am his shepherd, linked to
him Americanwise through Harlem,
through Peru, through Chad.

1976
What She Means

STILL-LIFE, WITH FRATERNITY

for Ted Grieder

In dream, enormous tree-house, led up to by a ladder, a hive of sorts,
the distance to the ground frightening.
In the top of the hive, bunk to bunk, the pledges and actives, like
    cakes
in an oven, all the same, or so we seem to me still, in the dream
    going on
then, a "still-life" but even if stilled, still life. Below,
as if hundreds of feet below, there were actives awake working
out an earlier dream — the pledges were to be aroused from sleep,
driven down the ladder and beaten at the base of the tree,
the tree-house fraternity contracting and expanding,
at one moment it is the frail one I built 15 feet over the sidewalk
    next to 4075
and then it is a relative mansion, my "Grand Central Station" where
I talk with my mother and try to keep out
of the dream a certain maniacal presence,
we are always at the bottom of a staircase
with simonized relatives slipping around us,
all oak, very wooden, warm at that base, a neurotic
launching-pad, deep in-firing cyst poised in the limbs or floating
high in the air, from which a root of smoke dangles

                                        I must descend
when they shout for me, as if I were ripped
from my Siamese twin

Below Dunn's farm where the frat fire plays,
Jay Christy is screwing Bunny MacCrory,
several months later he is out there alone,
I pull up, he wiggles out beer in hand, "Laura" is on the radio,
his girl-friend is sitting in the front seat in a wash basin
he found in the Phi Delt kitchen, her bottom
wet in abortioned ooze, Christy and I carry the basin behind his car,
look at it in my headlights, we can't tell if it's all come out yet.
We might as well have been looking into a mirror
or have been two stone lawn cherubs holding up a bird bath —
    the focus
belonged to the brotherhood, we were searching for pieces of flesh.
All rites of passage, whether well or poorly conducted,
bend the individual soul into the will of the nation or tribe,

and mine is the ghost back of Phi Delta Theta
screwing Bunny back into the woodwork out of which at
17 years old she timidly put forth her sex,
Christy fixes his screwdriver into her slot
he turns her back into matter
tosses the screwdriver into the trunk and walks away

What is virgin or just beginning to be experienced
is destroyed before it is fully there.
In ceremonies that pretended to carry us across
from being boys to being men the actual transition
was from a pledge trembling in bunny-footed p.j.s at a midnight
    "line-up"
to an active with a paddle pinned to a girl from a top
    sorority,
TV holding hands Saturday evening or when the weather was good
the frat fire at Dunn's farm with songs,
that maniacal presence where the pines began
as if our relative, Manson, wanted to join us, all bloody wanting
to be part of our evening

Bunny MacCrory, split under the force of the bore
regardless of how tentative it was,
now had an upper and a lower life,
now the tiny Phi Delt sword could be tucked
through her cashmere sweater nipping her bra
while her discolored lower parts cooked for us, the mammy in our
    basement,
or crouched behind the house in the bushes Sunday evening
willing to blow whoever found out she was there

What remains can be seen Sunday after church and Sunday
    dinner,
the pledges are kind of grubby, they have no time to do their own
    laundry,
the actives are imperial, they pose against the limestone or
toss footballs while the girls who are under them
wait. There is no time in this moment, the leaves'
shadow stops—the suits we are wearing, the utter
outerness of our lives translates itself out into our most inner
problems; we are not just kids wandering around in sport coats and
    ties,
we are our own aura, you can see in us at our edges supple
brown snake-skin shoes, Christy favors a sable brown brass buttoned
    blazer,

without any difficulty of transition we are models posed on phantom
    jets
for Harper's Bazaar 1965 "What America Does Best"
khaki wool tweed opening on a burst of orange.

1976
What She Means

THE COGOLLO

for Theodore Enslin

Driving back from your reading at Irvine,
knowing Reich's orgastic potency has become self-regulation for me
and I am stuck with it, a truth like a match a crow throws and
    lights
against the rock, they laugh "have a better orgasm!" ha ha
written as my mother used to, she did not know how to tell
    something funny,
ha ha the laughter of the billions who support love-yearn anxiety,
"gratified" they say, good orgasms yah, a moment later they are again
those billions gulping the sex bait, they say "orgasm"
as if that dim sublime makes up for the failure of two people
to create the sacred, moisten the atmosphere around them,
where the contradictions, the revilements, the self-doubt and self-pity
are burned, so that the elves and archai,
linked paperclips of energy, are revitalized in the air around us.
Having taken off our corsets and 19th century
headgear, how perplexing it is, to feel media
slipping the power out of language as one might bone
a chicken before the remaining flesh is roasted, eaten, done with,
and to realize too that Reich is but one aspect of a point
slowly being opened, a black spot in the lives of people 100 years ago
when childrens' hands were tied to bedposts at night
and husbands never once saw their wives naked,
when masturbation on the part of young girls was punished by
excising the girl's clitoris. *"You are so beautiful..."*
the radio crooned this afternoon, driving down Wilshire,
I was seeing the linked paperclips, realizing how they had become
spaceships for Reich, how beautiful that he had put
that much into the air, had given the air almost
what it had given him as he struggled into his 57th year
while the FDA spent 10% of its budget to feed him into prison and
    literally
break his heart. I hear in that crooning "beautiful"
the Nazi current running obliquely through America,
adoration of the flesh as a thing in itself,
Miss America turns on her platter, I see stadiums of Nazi
Youth stoned on calisthenics, their strong well-tended bodies
doing jumping jacks on a black
Indian's back, he is pulling

mussels from a baked field which are his dinner, I so free by
   comparison
walk into my bedroom and look at the unmade double pillowed bed
touched by the soft sculpture of a blanket poised in the bend Caryl
   left it
when she got up this morning to get dressed for work—*fidelity*
the most beautiful thing on earth, but do I convey it
using that radio word? How closely everything
is packed in spoonwise with its opposite, the grass
is full of Donald Duck, a cartoon of what everyone does to each
   other
doing ha ha to each other. Orgasm as gargoyle,
split spewer that juts from cathedral edge,
heretical companion; in the tension of the missing orgasm
men created Paradise and they stand in circle,
a huge wall around that gap focusing their rage
on its most precious human contrary, a pussy
white and frightened leaps around before them like a bunny.
Men live at a never ending sexual funeral
where their ripped-away Siamese twin is the stuff in the casket,
when they look closely he is the remains of a Paleolithic
bison, their real double, their 50% other, the animal
they lost in their cavity when eons ago they descended
the pyramid's inner stairway to become ha ha immortal.
Knowing remains a procedure
instead of the knower revealing the process through which
his living is connected to what he knows, yet
the cogollo, "the heart of the cabbage, the shoot of the plant,
the summit of pine" need not be missing.
At the core of my poetry, where my mother is buried,
I dream the strength of my yearning toward oneness,
when the critics of the day
become the succubi of 4 AM
I think them aside and conserve my strength for the morning.
Love, made, keeps me living in the poem and the poem,
to remain pregnant in birth, tumbles me out on the shore
to illuminate, with Caryl again, antiphonal.

1976
What She Means

SCORPION HOPSCOTCH

Unexpectedly this morning I grasped
my orgasm and held it for a moment in my hands,
outwardly a crystal ball—yet as I looked
I penetrated my own reflection and glimpsed
its marvelous inner workings, death
was happy there, a gold fluid that streamed
through the crystal complexity of what I saw,
happy because without orgasm it was forced
to hammer at my back, as if I were death's door.
Around death's fluid were many tiny insects,
flies, spiders, even little grubs who seemed to be
nursing at the teats of what is passing through—
they gave death a furry quality, made it more solid
feeling, as if what I see of nature outside of orgasm
was nourished by invisible death—but it was not as if death
"lurked" in the act as Berdyaev and Bataille have said,
a scorpion to sting the lovers when they open that wide,
but flashed across what seemed to be a winning line, as if death
won a race then that otherwise had it pounding at my back,
and around the insects a feeling of mooing, a low animal
sound density that pressed against the crystal limits,
inhabiting them in a kind of roller coaster rhythm,
an animal cushion, sharp, breathless and slow, between
the nursing insects and the sudden
reappearance of our bedroom.

1976
What She Means

"for your father" she said,
and then, "how dedicate a book to
someone who is dead?"
Lavender dusk all over the dining-room windows,
I left making steak tartare, walked out on the porch.
No lavender. All inside. Rose hued,
rhyming with the plum brandy I used in the tartare.
Bach Cantata #93 as we ate. Outside
the royal palm had not been touched,
a cement collar, apartment backed,
pastelled, he is stronger now, an old tree
living in this neighborhood—
suppose him across the street
watching me, thinking about Gladys,
a peculiar tree, he will never rhyme
with another man. Tom Meyer said that when he, Jonathan,
and a third man get into bed,
a fourth as presence seemed to be beside the bed,
then I thought: the denied woman?
a wraith in semen-rags weeping by the post?
I will always put a woman in his place
because he did not seem to want one.
A cap on a ladder chipping paint,
or shoulders over his vise by the furnace.
Other. Did not rhyme with my mother. Or if he did,
the rhyme was so gentle my unmatching hands
would never feel it in substance.
I kneaded the raw meat
and thought about the sparrows in his crown.
Friday night. A disappointing shade—
but: he was not a hammer. He did not,
as did the men of Idi Amin, force me to pound
a dead man's head to pulp and then put
my head in it for the night. There was no one to kill,
no corpse to be fucked over—
therefore Tantrik stenography is for me unreal?
After Caryl there is only the earth, and
with her once I put myself through her into the earth,
held on to vines for my dear life.
A sunset along the Hudson later, as strange
as this light tonight. But when I went to see him,

at the slaughterhouse, having waited years,
there was only a man at a desk in a large room
with fifty men at desks. This is my son, he said,
to a few of them. Then: well, I guess I'm ready to go.
A few yards away the slaughterhouse
where for years he had walked, on planks I believe,
in his white smock. *Mr. Belvedere —*
time and motion study. A man watching
a four-way meat clock,
loin chimes, a horn dial,
an animal tick. Nothing got revealed,
nothing was shown. I gather
he was nearly impotent. Why?
When a gang of men tumble into bed
is he the shade by the post?
Blind. With swan's breasts,
perhaps holding a candle, as if
by that light something of the way
people really do things
would become visible?
He is very old and only a small part of him
is in any way mine. My mother noticed that
when she turned over on her side.
Lights out. Crickets. The porch swing still
by the screened morning glories.
Sure she is asleep, he gets up for a glass of warm water.
Stands by the living-room drapes.
If I could have known for one moment
what he was thinking. About his fire-cracker?
He gave me a hollow
in which to fit, and since I did not,
he fell to ash. Yet never completely.
But one of his clock motions must be called ash.
Bright snow on the lawn. What
was he really thinking? About his cornet?
It is too easy to know. I want to transmit
transformed memory. I want to inhabit
him for a moment, be his figure of woman.
Maybe it is him at Tom's bedpost,
the old man thinking about something like a woman.
That vague. Warmed by the throaty men
he is unsure whether they are fucking or fighting.
They warm him. That is what counts,
no matter that they appear to be flames
and he thinks he stands by the bay window.
No father knows where he is. As long

as he is a father. When he is father, I
am his girlfriend Olive Oil. Cemetery
romance. The American sublime. The men
are coated with snow, he watches the front-
yard writhe, his wife's head in hair net,
the three men hug and make
an odd pose of her face. He drinks,
as if at a trough. The age tastes of blood.
He is free to walk into the kitchen.
How hungry he is. He peeks into the refrigerator,
it is crammed with alive cattle. He wants
to experience something that is not
father. Father, he says to his own,
pour me a glass of dandelion wine!
And that is the cage. That his father is
locked in too. And the mothers
unawakenable. Why? I have to keep asking.
Why, why, let it press father into
father into ice where only a bison
might be observing. The mothers
are down in the earth with steel in their ears.
The sisters and brothers are even further away.
So why does this father not visit me?
Why does he remain uncertain before men?
Why does he not know that the men in bed
are not hurting one another?
Why doesn't he know they are there
instead of in a cockpit or in uniform?
My father grows older and older by the drapes.
At times I think he has left. Then I creep from my room,
afraid of being scolded,
but since I am older too,
his scold would be a kind of toast.
I knead the meat, unsure of why I am eating it raw.
Was it male too? This is being lost
like I have never allowed him to be before.
An old man necking with himself in a parked car.
A father reaching directly into ice.
Insubstantial. Deer father the poets cry.
Snail father. Father in some form.
Why have you become insubstantial
right at the moment deer woman has thrown off
her fake antlers? Why do you disappear
right as she walks from the deer?
Why do I not know why I am here?
On the personal level alone my father turns to me

and then an earthquake turns,
or the moon, he comes and can be viewed.
But the tripod is broken,
the alligator frame is missing.
Here for the breath of erasure, that's why.

1976
What She Means

STILL-LIFE, WITH AFRICAN VIOLETS

The little pot of them in the Beverly
Hills flower shop window,
purple sable, sand, African
violence, a crazed very black
man shouting at the flower shop,
Africa pulled up to within feet of
Beverly Drive, he shouts from sand and luster, sweating,
but from the flower shop he just moves his mouth, he is dirty,
hysterical, he is waving a hoe, the clerks
glance at the window sometimes, a siren or
customer's nose presses against
the African violets on their mind,
nothing moves, begins to squirm
between the hoarse African and the neat lady clerk,
nothing finally starts to move, the air
so packed with everything the African has neglected to do,
the lady clerk looks down at
the straw in her soda, thinks of God, how silly, sucks
at the frothy bottom, the African rolls over on his mat,
the pain in his anus will hardly let him hoe, the night is not
death rich with the transformational mesh of sky and field,
but skinny with death, white goons in jeeps drip
from his brow, he picks up a handful of dust,
nostalgic gesture, the lady clerk is nostalgic gesture,
if they were both smeared on a rock he
would be denser, she would be mucilage, a bird
would stay by his smear longer, nothing thinks
this is very funny, that part of my mind touched by nothing,
soft frayed earlaps of violets,
nothing surrounds them, crushes them when it throws a fit,
yet since all of us are in social time
I will not try to balance myself on nothing,
I will believe the enraged African is thicker
than the Beverly Hills lady clerk, in doing so I will betray
my own life a block south of Beverly Hills,
my physical body is here with the retail violet instead of with
the violet in the earth; I want him to smash the jeep goon,
but I better be willing to deal with the black man when he
kills the goons, especially when I saw one of their white hands,
just a second ago, come in the window and take hold of my left
    wrist,

I shook it off with a chill, a floral chill, the embroidery of a fangy
white African hand with purple veins touched my wrist to caution
    me
No way to take sides and to think at the same time,
you either allow both that black and that clerk to be in contradiction
or you pass into a thinness, your word must be
at least as thick with sand and sable, dry animal
tongue out, the terrified goon's neck cradled,
sliced, desperate lizard, fly trapped between screen and window,
say "African violet" and Pandora begins to twitch her goat feet,
the mutiny that tickles nothing begins to stir and then yawns before
your corrected feelings . . . So is the point to strengthen
the glass between us to the point that nothing feels pinched
and begins to abandon us? How? By a good deed? By sweating in
    our
imaginations? By breaking up the altar glass near the end
of our minds, where the religious explanations sit
attentive and foreveresque in blue uniforms with gunpowder braid?
How does an African with a hoe do that? He hits a tree, he
hits his kid, I mentalize a terrifying lode of world in Beverly Hills
African violets, but our acts are not the same, *Oh yes they are*
Pan squeaks from the molecule in which he is trapped, the
    atmosphere is
now so packed with nothing there is no real difference between a slap
and a wince of perception, an animal starts down a dusty glass path,
think of her as a tear running a flower shop window or as a disease
shaped like a cougar boiling with a craze for release,
you will only yoke this beast by traveling as a tear in these other
wills, you will need the protection a tear ball can give you,
a head, feeling the outpack of the air, striations of nothing like
    gossamer
red veins in the air, pull them down and that fancy white hand will
    again
clutch your arm, lucky man, leave them be and the same force may
maggot your width, you are where repetition is parallel to itself,
clutch-clutch, meaning Animal why don't you get to where you are
    going,
you, animal, you, black cougar with lady clerk spectacles, you, fly
with paws, boiling to release nothing, to see the extent of the silage
in the depths of nothing, a compost — or billions of howling beings?
You got a wink of them at Hiroshima and you actually touched
your portion of their skin at Yunotsu, you sat in green mineral
water in which the hives of burning were large as frogs, now
break in hell as well as heaven, see them in goosestep before your
    eyes,
fly which is a cougar suffering, eating its hoe behind the rich peoples'

114

flower shop, an inch behind your head, where you dwell with Sammy
Davis Jr., in the same porcelain cup poised on the descendingly
   atrocious
ant-hill-like living strata suckled by that meek mold, nothing.

1977
What She Means

THE NAME ENCANYONED RIVER

Hello and farewell, César Vallejo, at the margin of
your name encanyoned river, complete,
yet utterly rushing away, the bottom is dry
and in motion, enchased, liquor
pounding at its casket sides, buried treasure
half afloat in sand, translating is a child's
game, there is nothing in that ornate chest,
pirates are stumps set on quicksand,
translating is a man's name, pirates are rapists,
the cabin shudder emits its Dachau
whistle, what is inside the name?
For fifteen years you have rivered my sleep,
as if I slept under your gun,
as if my dreams took place in the pipe
you flowed through, language
can weigh you, tell how much you are
other, how much you were
ego, you flow dust
between Indian presence and Catholic presence,
a Marxist conundrum, the heir is endless
as well as the variations on what I can see, a text
is a staircase leading down into a vault
where a man with a face like a turnip explains
through teeth-knotted gums that he is neither coward
nor hero, neither the king I expected to find in my tomb
nor the slave I passed in the toilet, but a composition
I was redoing out of my desire to realize
another, happened to be called César Vallejo,
leaving tracks I followed, in deepest
sincerity, around the stone
now articulate in Caryl's gaze,
which then disappears down the gullet of the dead snake gnawer,
alone in the flesh vale, beyond the lights of the carnival,
that groin we met in, anxiety
over the weight of the infant cowl in each dawn
and the elderly scrawl in each sunset, a penis with
its chicken head shot off. You were to sleep in my dream
when my urge was blocked by maggots,
you appeared a dead hobo between Barbara and myself,
your marble face insapphired crystal,
a river frozen between ego and other

my senses could not thaw
until I wept into you, got my tears in hand,
a cry for the infant of occasion to break
through the back-turned linoleum of the hardened present
world, as if the discussion were *What shall we eat*
and took place in the kitchen, instead of *Why most do not*
which churns in the thyroid of television,
life is up to you, they say, and how you feel
cutting up a TV set for dinner, a problem of translation,
the Vietnamese peasant whose blown apart head,
dots on the screen, still disengages, verbs, adjectives,
pieces of linkage of cosmic creatures,
irreflective puddles at the foot of a shattered tree,
the lager is despair, pools which lie around each
turn of mind "but you knew it was self-reflection,
so why did you expect a bridge?"
That voice—from where does it come?
From the reader, of course, in a plane,
a concerned academic friend, who glimpses me below
tangled in the landing gear, covered with Entebbe or some other
horrible occasion, death as the ground of inspiration
but so far below and so total, I fly with talons in my back
while my feet stroll on a ball-bearinged earth.
Dragged from soil to soil each person knows,
if only at near orgasm, archeological strata is the dirty
gossip, the obscene penetration. Nature and God
tunnel us, stone smoothing gadgets, our value
increases as the edges become more porous,
again I am inside the Temple of Inscriptions,
dazzled by the ornate sarcophagus lid,
"The grandeur is all back there!" it shouts,
muffled by the heat of the jungle around us,
"And all here!" the skeleton beginning to breathe
between the tall neighboring trunks
rubs and whines. In the back-drawer of the imagination and
the frontal narrowness of perception
I went to your wall, I gave it drink,
the wail drank, the wall opened its mouth
stone, then split, its gullet shone like mink,
I am the mother crying a chain to
the daughter behind bars, you are the grandfather
in whose hand suffering is softness untranslated,
the steel muck between the text and the poet's
desire to know what his sex
wants to inhabit, who fears the air of what
he has seen, who tears apart his own tears

to know the minute monolithic weight of the mists,
his fathers, swirling towards him, as if he owed
them anything, for they are his compost
which has suddenly had the nerve to speak!
Our pores are full in each bud, each
a little bath speared by the air, they
deepen yoked to the soft yellow they sag in,
multivarious influences, anxiety
was the base until the ego recoiled on its stem.
Connection and correspondence must be allowed to
abide, kill, mutate and progress,
organs die and revivify, die
and misdirect, through the glass-bottomed text
your opaqueness still swims,
daddy-long-legs sport in the topsoil and the critic
is a condition of not enough poetry
heard when the parents are evaluated.
My writing is air-conditioned over
the breasts of Beverly Hills anxieties,
Jesus mounted on Darwin's turtle, on whose shell is written:
hello and farewell, rib of Kyoto, on which the core
meander was not Bashō but Vallejo, slug
which finding itself at the bottom of the kitchen sink,
late at night, disappeared back through the drain,
worked its way through the maze of the Cross to
the roots of the fig tree to climb its trunk and be seen,
in morning sunlight, motionless on the stump
of a hacked off branch. At the point in the imagination
where an answer is begged for,
there is sweat, ikons belong to the religious.
My joy in the literal was to believe in you,
not misuse you as my own blocked worksheet.
The apprentice contacts a realized other,
he has a choice to encircle or
to glue himself to the other's mirror,
the other, when first contacted,
turns his back a wall of stone,
the apprentice scratches red dots,
signs of menstrually blessed vegetable patches,
his Cro-Magnon torque to be in history:
mirror me, but double the mirror,
mirror my actual reflection but steam what I am
with the lie of myself I seek to erase,
give me the bread of your tensions, not their crusts,
for I am a greedy pig converting your table into a trough,
the apprentice must demand and demand and demand, not

of the outward man, but the ticks and
the worms of which what is mastered is composed,
crowned ticks and worms in long queenly gowns that were,
in the process of being mastered, crumbling bark and loam,
stuff that appears to endlessly repeat itself, a handful of weeds
or moments of desire which in their infinitely complex nature
appear to be minute cathedrals in which sea-urchins are worshipping,
where wolves are handling the Book of Psalms, moments in which
the freedom of movement wears a lush religious gown,
and this gown when looked at carefully is composed of one-eyed
    jacks,
and then of black and white rags, and finally of bare kneelings,
the poor before a Jesus candle while the switches of the parents
swing through the censorial smoke, these are the moments when
    desire
if not confronted encloses the apprentice in a diving-bell,
the back of the master may still be at work in the flood
but the diving-bell rolls free and becomes a beautifully curtained cage,
a stage coach in which the aged apprentice is riding,
a grandfather clock ticks away before him in his compartment,
its ornate face is closed, a lid over a mechanism
that magnetizes the past in all things, trees flash by and he
thinks of a childhood walk with a flashlight he had shone up a trunk,
he failed to puncture himself, he did not escape Aladdin's fate,
he is no longer an apprentice, yet he is, a guest in the backward
reflecting bottle shape of poetry, an aging homunculus hearing
in each clippity-clop the om-coated mice by his own bitter toes.
Vallejo, in my simultaneous farewellello, the split-level
existence, the male poet caught between mush and glass, was
shattered; facing the height of your contradiction I tore the moss
out of the kingly sockets of the Temple of Inscriptions.
From moment to moment I stand in the socket itself and see the
    socket for what it is,
a butterfly socket, a basin of stone, again and again I must erase
this central mirror, the closet I experience in living
in which I seek to put on my mother's girdle
and appear a likable goy before my friends,
the closet in which I put on my friends' lies
and seek to appear an appropriate bride for my father!
Concentrated by your flesh, I transferred my inner gold to
my surface iron, I saw the task was to live in the amplitude
of contradiction, not in the deathhouse of male versus female
desire; "parasite" is now clear: the poet
must grip into his own caterpillar,
as the caterpillar he must expel his digger-wasp,
his White Anglo night crawler which slips

between his sheets, shyly asking for mercy
while it deposits ikons in all his inkwells.
Still vital in poetry is the belief that the master can
keep his back turned and his vulnerability present,
that the apprentice will have the strength
to reflect that back until he gives himself mind.
This is why one should want to live,
not to break oneself into children, but,
off the back of one's chosen backing,
to become a mirror, absorb, break, and be porous,
then assimilate the mirror one has chosen, hold
the essence of reflection, as long as one can,
then shake that dear prey, once one's master,
once big as the world, out of one's fingers . . .
Personal is released from confessional ties,
the conspiracy in world poetry against a person
openly and imaginatively working with what has happened to him
is the terror of the fathers, what I felt muted
in the overgrown lot next to 4705,
the soft stomach of the poem
made to believe that its navel is vile;
personal is not private, person is what accrues to me,
the personal is a volatile exchange, the nose of the fish
and its gills as well, I only really advance open and eaten by
what passes into/out of me, I am the poem with a focus
disturbed yet happy with my pilot fish, ancient Cross
is to say its arms out and head on, to endure the tension of
puberty not as a mantle but as the eye at the end of the vault
in which a cherry tree is blooming, zero is a lasso this tree knows,
each of its jade and pink blossoms is aglow with nature and
with God, cradling its river, encanyoning lingam and yoni,
not as ikons but as flexions, the process known as Vallejo
insapphires and unties the glistening hocker
of Indiana, scrawled on a diner toilet wall:
"A little bird with golden bill / perched on my windowsill;
I fed him crumb and crust of bread / then smashed his fucking head."
Hail and farewell, César Vallejo, I collect this gravel
from the plate glass of your back, I am your widower,
dearest created brother, until the healthy legs
are surrounded by the resurrection of the lame.

1977
What She Means

120

THE LICH GATE

Waiting, I rest in the waiting gate.
Does it want to pass my death on
or to let my dying pass into the poem?
Here I watch the windshield redden
the red of my mother's red Penney coat,
the eve of Wallace Berman's 50th birthday drunk
truck driver smashed Toyota,
a roaring red hole, a rose in whirlpool
placed on the ledge of a bell-less shrine.
My cement sits propped against the post. To live
is to block the way and
to move over at the same time, to hang
from the bell-less hook, a tapeworm in the packed
organ air, the air resonant with fifes, with mourners
filing by the bier
resting in my hands, my memory coffer
in which an acquaintance is found.
Memory is acquaintance. Memory is not a friend.
The closer I come to what happened,
the less I know it, the more occasionally I love
what I see beyond the portable
frame in which I stand—I, clapper, never free,
will bang, if the bell rope is pulled.
Pull me, Gladys and Wally say to my bell, and you
will pass through, the you of I, your
pendulum motion, what weights
you, the hornet-nest shaped
gourd of your death, your scrotal
lavender, your red red glass crackling
with fire-embedded mirror. In vermilion and black
the clergyman arrives. At last
something can be done about this
weighted box. It is the dead who come forth to
pull it on. I do nothing here.
When I think I do, it is the you-hordes
leaning over my sleep with needle-shaped
fingers without pause they pat
my still silhouette which shyly moves.
The lich gate looks like it might collapse.
Without a frame in which to wait,
my ghoul would spread. Bier in lich,

Hades' shape, his sonnet prism reflecting
the nearby churchyard, the outer hominid limit,
a field of rippling meat. I have come here
to bleed this gate, to make my language fray
into the invisibility teeming against
the Mayan ballcourt of the Dead, where
I see myself struggling intently,
flux of impact, the hard rubber
ball bouncing against the stone hoop.

1979
Hades in Manganese

III
THE SEPARATION CONTINUUM

PLACEMENTS I

for Jerome Rothenberg

Anguish, a door, Le Portel, body bent over jagged rock, in ooze, crawling in dark to trace the button of itself—or to unbutton the obscure cage in which a person and an animal are copulas—or are they delynxing each other? Or are they already subject and predicate in the amniotic cave air watching each other across the word barrier, the flesh?

*

At arm's length the image, my focus the extent of my reach. Where I end the other begins. Is not all art that genuinely moves us done in the "dark" against a "wall"? Olson's whisper (a prayer), "boundary, disappear."

*

I squat in my mother's arch, eating, the black beckons so I go, crawling to I know not where. The terror of crawling within my own shoulder space is exceeded by the instinct that I might fully crawl out of the frame my mother dimensioned me with—but to continue is finally to return, doubled back on my umbilical possibility. It is on the way back that I scratch what might be thought of as the fact that since I ceased being an animal, I have not known what to do with myself.

*

The beginning of the construction of the underworld takes place in Upper Paleolithic caves. To identify this "place under construction," I use the later Greek word "Hades," and it is there that the first evidence of psyche that we can relate to occurs. To be in the cave is to be inside an animal—a womb—but to draw there is to seek another kind of birth: an adjustment to the crisis of the animal separating out of the human—or, the Fall. To be inside, to be hidden, to be in Hades—where the human hides in the animal.

*

Since the hidden is bottomless, totality is more invisible than visible. Insistence on a totality in which life is totally visible is the anti-dream. Hades deprived of his depths, Satan attempting to establish a kingdom—or death camp—solely on earth.

*

It took thousands and thousands of years, but we did create the abyss out of a seemingly infinite elastic crisis: therio-expulsion—and we have lived in a state of "animal withdrawal" ever since. The pictures in the abyss that flicker our sleep and waking are the fall-out that shouted us into dot and line and from which we have been throwing up and throwing down ever since. What we project as abyss, and into it, are the guardians, or sides of boundary, the parietal labor to bear Hermes, to give a limit to evasiveness, to contour meandering, to make connections.

*

As species disappear, the Upper Paleolithic grows more vivid. As living animals disappear, the first outlines become more dear, not as reflections of a day world, but as the primal contours of psyche, the shaping of the underworld, the point at which Hades was an animal. The "new wilderness" is thus the spectral realm created by the going out of animal life and the coming in, in our time, of these primary outlines. Our tragedy is to search further and further back for a common non-racial trunk in which the animal is not separated out of the human while we destroy the turf on which we actually stand.

1978
Hades in Manganese

HADES IN MANGANESE

for James Hillman

Today I'd like to climb the difference
between what I think I've written and
what I *have* written, to clime being,
to conceive it as a weather
generate and degenerate,
a snake turning in digestion with the low.

But what you hear
are the seams I speak, animal,
the white of our noise
meringues into peaks
neither of us mount—or if we do,
as taxidermists, filling what is over
because we love to see as if alive.

Seam through which I might enter,
wounded animal, stairwayed
intestine in the hide of dream,
Hades, am I
yule, in nightmare
you weigh my heart,
you knock, in the pasture at noon,
I still panic
awaking at 3 AM
as if a burglar were in the hall,
one who would desire me, on whose claw
I might slip a ring, for in the soft
cave folds of dream
in conversation you woo, I weigh,
I insert something cold in you,
you meditate me up, I carry
what is left of you, coils
of garden hose, aslant, in my gut . . .

Hades, in manganese you rocked, an animal,
the form in which I was beginning to
perish, wading in eidola
while I separated you out!
To cross one back line with
another, hybrid, to take from the graft
the loss, the soul now wandering
in time, thus grieving for

what it must invent, an out of time,
an archetype, a non-existing
anthrobeast, rooted and seasonally
loosing its claws in the air!

O dead living depths!
One face cooing to another plungers
that went off, torpedos, in dream,
to spin through a pasture at noon,
sphincter-milled, sheep-impacted,
the lower body attached
to separation, pulling the seam of it along
cold cave stone, the head as
a pollen-loaded feeler tunneling
to ooze a string of eggs
where the rock, strengthening its yes,
returned the crawler to vivid green
sunlight that *was* profundity
now invested with linkage,
the grass, invested with linkage,
the whole sky, a tainted link,
man, a maggot on stilts,
desiring to leave elevation at the mouth
to seam unyield to his face.
Tethered, Hades phoned, om
phallos, the metro the zipper
of dread at every branch-off,
the pasture at noon conducted
by the bearmarm below, batoning
sun down word rust scraper by scraper out.

        *

Below, in the culvert
behind the house of Okumura, Kyoto, 1963,
the conveyor-belt ran all night.
The clanking got louder, tore
then died, surf roar, origin beguiling,
a highway was going through.
During late night breaks,
the itinerant laborers would smoke
by a sparking oil drum in domed yellow helmets,
navy-blue wool puttees, men goblined by metal,
pitch blackness and popping fire. I watched
from a glassed-in porch, not quite able to see
inside the drum, wanting to engage

the action, to tie the fire into a poem
Paul Blackburn spoke on tape to me,
which would not burn. He suffered savage men,
without a context, standing about a dying fire
jacking off into it. Depth was the crisis
I tried to raise. The surf roar, earth
tearing, lifted, but not transformed, seemed,
as if part of me, an unending mechanicality.
I could and could not—it could and could.

I was, in spirit, still
in puberty, before my typewriter,
as if in a pew before an altar,
itchy, bored, afraid of being whipped
when we all got home. I played the hymnals
and black choir gowns into a breathing cellar
larder, a ladder to
convincing ore, a bed-shaped
Corregidor flashing, as if a beacon, to me adrift
—or was it the Phi Delta Theta dorm door opened
a crack? I would think of Mrs. Bird's canary
waiting to be driven downstairs and beat bloody.
That canary, hardly an image, helped me,
but it faded in an instant, the actives were
shouting around our bunks, beating pans.
Meowing like Raoul Hausmanns—or were we silent?—
we bent over where the wall had been removed
and only the fireplace remained, gripping
each others' shoulders, our naked huddle
encircled the open-ended fire—we were fisted
loosely to a turbined mass, our heads
a common tampax clamped into the actives' hate.

This fire surrounded by walls of flesh is now
contained. Hades makes a target of this maze.

                    *

Perseus holds the written head out to the sun.
His sword from his hip projects what is on his mind,
a center torn from a center, Medusa
wrenched from her jellyfish stronghold,
her severed pipes, the caterwauling serpents,
his treasure from the underworld.
The hero will not be
transfixed into himself, he will lift

reflected terror from reflected depth,
he will thrust his hand down
into the sodden tampax mass where earth bleeds.
My father, for 30 years timing blacks
slaughtering steers, folds into men
beating the animal in other men,
extracting its Pan-pipes, jugular flutes of morning.

Picking the confetti from our hair,
Little Lulu and I cross the city
Francis Bacon mayors. In this city
cartoons mingle equally with men.
In their cruel goo outlines I sense
the terrible strength in our lifting up,
unceasingly to translate upward,
to take whatever stuff and lift it,
earth, dream, whatever, up,
the pyramidic impulse to slave-point sunward,
to streamline, rather than to learn from, Lazarus.

    *

Surface is reality as is ascension
as is depth. Medusa hangs down through
fathoms of archaic familiarity,
the pylons men have made of female psyche,
women beat into gates through which to draw
the ore of heroic energy, to appease
a masculine weather for manipulation and torture.
War on matter lumped into a procrustian mater
crammed, with her crucified familiar,
into the entrance way to Hades. I knew,
holding my 50 pound mother in her swaddling
cancer sheet, that there is no triumph *over*.
Resurrection, a Carl Dreyer altarpiece, yes,
a true finger-exercise in hope, a waist-
hinge, in the waste of spirit the crocus-bud
surely is not to be denied, its yellowy flame
playing among the stones warms what is
youngest in us, most held in night, tender,
voracious for sunset, fire appetite,
to watch the mountain smoke with modesty,
the thing to transform itself, lifting
from itself but carrying Hades as pendulum,
the parachutist gathering in Medusa's threads,

an intelligence under, not of us, but receptive
to us as we drift and wither . . .

Why do we treat the hero
better than he treated the material
he severed to feed the sun?
Perseus with his fistful of belladonna,
could we transform him into a hermit
with a lantern? Give him an awl,
teach him meander-work, zigzag wobbling through
the infante-clotted rushes, teach him salamander,
teach his semen how to stimulate fire. Unblock
the entrance way to Hades, allow the violet odors
of its meats to simmer in ice penetrating
advice. Something will work its magic against
the door of never. Hell Week, 1953,
a postcard Hades mailed to me,
his kids in demon suits tied to a string
about my penis led up through my white shirt
tied to a "pull me" card dangling
from my sport-coat pocket. The personal
is the apex of pain, but without it
mountains begin to numb specificity.
The personal works in specificity like a tail-
gunner, the tension in the dog-fight tying
my death into my work.

                    *

Concentration now includes Dachau,
barbed wire has replaced reason
as the circumference of energy. There is
no hail to rise to. Names are cultural
foam, nada-maggots stretching their scrawl-souls, paw
scorings in the frost of the mother corridor
where our faces were first ironed softly.

Hades receives meandering Hermes
mazing my thoughts into the La Pieta
softness of the target-maker's arms—
there what I change is ended, my despair
is nursed cryptically, for Hades' breasts,
like cob-webbed mangers, are miracleproof.
There a sucking goes on, below the obstructed
passage way, all senses of the word, stilled
in its being, take place. I am playing

with what is left of my animal, a marble
it rolls into neuter, a cat's eye, rolls back,
I crack its pupil between word-infant lips . . .

Bird spirit flew into Apollo —
animal appeared in Dis.
What was sky and earth became life and death,
or hell on earth and psychic depth,
and I wonder: how has Hades been affected by Dachau?
In the cold of deepest bowels, does a stained
fluid drip? Does pure loss now have an odor
of cremation, a fleshy hollow feel
of human soul infiltrating those realms
Hades had reserved for animals?
Are there archai, still spotted with
this evening's russets, stringing and quartering
an anthrobestial compost? Or are the zeros,
of which we are increasingly composed,
folding out the quick of animal life?
Is that why these outlines, these Hadic kin,
take on mountainous strength,
moving through the shadows of these days?

A wheeled figure stabs and sews
the infancy in our grain to the skin of the ground.
Wheeled wall master who mends in manganese,
talk through what I do not remember,
the life in which I am glued
stringings of narrative Ariadnes.
All hominids share a scarlet where the dark is
pitch with horizon, note leaps, the static
of non-meaning tendrilling us, making way
for not another bringing of the dark
up into the light, but a dark
delivered dark Paleolithic dimension.

1979
Hades in Manganese

SILENCE RAVING

Patters, paters, Apollo globes, sound
breaking up with silence, coals
I can still hear, entanglement of sense
pools, the way a cave would leak perfume —

in the Cro-Magnons went, along its wet hide walls,
as if a flower, way in, drew their leggy
panspermatic bodies, spidering over
bottomless hunches, groping toward Persephone's
fate: to be quicksanded by the fungus pulp of
Hades' purple hair exploding in their brains.

They poured their foreheads into the coals and corrals
zigzaged about in the night air,
                    the animals led in crossed
a massive vulva incised before the gate,
the power that came up from it was paradise, the power
the Cro-Magnons bequeathed to us, to make an altar of our throats.

The first words were mixed with animal fat,
wounded men tried to say who did it.
The group was the rim of a to-be-invented wheel,
their speech was spokes, looping over,
around, the hub of the fire, its silk of *us,*
its burn of *them,* bop we dip, you dip,
we dip to you, you will dip to us, Dionysus
the plopping, pooling words, stirred
by the lyre gaps between the peaks of flame,
water to fire, us to them.

Foal-eyed, rubbery, they looped
back into those caves whose walls could be strung
between their teeth, the sticky soul material pulled
to the sides by their hands, ooh
what bone looms they sewed themselves into, ah
what tiny male spiders they were
on the enormous capable of devouring them
female rock elastic word!

1979
Hades in Manganese

133

MASTER HANUS TO HIS BLINDNESS

Inside Staranova Synagogue,
deeply recessed stained glass,
such tender colors, pastel pinks, greens,
hammocked with cobwebs,
the slump in Czech character draped
by the Soviet net, the impenetrable dusk
our headlights could not shine through,
coal mine dusk, Borinage ghost of van Gogh,
a grimed religious body on straw
trying to worship its spirit up.

Imagine a living coal mine veined
across the land, streets finely
fissured with soot, a net become membrane,
a marbelization of the spirit
to which each particle of the burned
contributes. One says: the Soviet net,
then one smells and tastes the net!
A waiter explains why the menu's
suprème de volaille was, served,
chopped Chinese chicken: "Our people know
this is suprème de volaille."
Under the net, in ways hidden to me,
what *do* they know? Has the truth
in the life line marbelized lies?

Stunned before the vagueness of the sinister,
one's mind seeks out the physical world,
as if the mallards meandering the greasy Vltava
outside the botel porthole
had something to do with "better."

"Don't start feeling sorry for a Czech,"
Milan cautioned, "or you'll never stop."

     *

It is as if to think on Czechoslovakia
is to extend the soot, to describe
sensations, to participate in
a totalitarianism of imagination

which is description, the literal
ruling out the shades of place.
But if some facts are not given,
how can Master Hanus' address to his blindness
be understood? If the reader does not know
Hanus' beautiful astrological clock, know
that Hanus was blinded by Prague people
so that he could never duplicate the clock,
how could Hanus' words, spoken to me
in a coffee-shop, after I had seen the clock,
be understood?

    *

Poets in Czechoslovakia are deprived of expressing
their pain, are made to lie to publish.
Where does the pain go that they are not expressing?
In the same way that I cannot forgive
the Nazis because I was not in their camps,
I cannot know the pain of deprived expression.
I can embrace Jan and Milan and feel
the extent to which the bow has been drawn
and sense the filings in the soot
collecting along the unsent arrow shaft.
I know another kind of pain,
the anxiety that comes from knowing anything
can be said, that cutting into is merely shaving,
the poet as a kind of barber,
sanding the druidic off the giant,
who considers who is to live in Viet-X.
You cannot speak versus
you can say anything and it does not matter.
What is not permitted
gnaws at the ears of those
through whom the able-to-speak
passes without effect.

Does the ineffable lie between?
Palm on a tree crotch by the ocean
Rilke felt the other side of nature
as a quiet, steeling bliss.
The other side of nature . . .
Fear introjected until the mind gags.
Shadow streets cheered
by eyes cowled with *I suffer like you* . . .

*

"For making time beautiful, I have been
pressed to time, toll
of the maggots stretching in my sockets.
By the ledge of the Vltava,
the heels of my palms press in stars,
chubby star worms unable to display
their energies along these poplar-lined banks.
I made a harp of time, and hang
from its strings which they drew
through my eyes, a stilled pendulum
against the other side of human nature."

*

At the combined press of Rilke's and Hanus' palms,
something moves bliss to terror,
cancelling both, a kind of blister
in which a man in a Tusex store is trying to buy
his child something he does not need
with foreign money he cannot have,
a fistless man in a room without windows.

1979
Hades in Manganese

EQUAL TIME

Somehow it seems wrong,
a minute on Vietnam refugees
at sea, starving, not allowed to
dock, followed by a minute
on a new world's record in cherry
pit spitting, wrong because
the pit record trivializes a human
plight — so, should we dwell
on an imagined deck, imagined
cries? Somehow the dwelling itself
seems wrong, not only being here
but dwelling on what thought does
not alter. Or on what thought only
raises as thought, say my presenting
suffering to you as language
instead of handing you an actual
refugee. The baby hare
my son and I found had
abscessed legs, so we set it back
in its tall grass. Its tremble
brings the refugees closer, its being
alone, frightened, defenseless,
might enter the champion
cherry pit spitter's mind as
he dreams in a structure that includes
an altered sense of language
that must include the desert
mountains this morning not as part
of the news but of the evolving net
writing poetry throws out,
wanting to include, hesitant to
look back, knowing violence and
the moral impossibility of balancing
the refugees, the pit champ and the hare —
or is the poem to fictionalize such
a balance, is it to hang each with a counterbalancing
weight so that, clearly unequal, they
float over to an immense ear, an Ithacan
grotto, as the magical things upon which
the homecome wanderer rests his head?
It is too easy in a world that refuses dockage

to refugees to play on the spit out pit,
to allow the Odysseus of one's imagination
to rest for more than a moment on
an archetypal pillow in which hare,
champ and refugee are bees, producing
a distinct but unified Mass, an edible
hosea, a surge toward a drooping prophesied head
from which flows a common honey
— *tu viens, chéri?* This structure
must include a sweetness in bed
as well as the mascara in the coffin-
deep rue St.-Denis doorway where the empty
champ touches the abscessed refugee,
where he mounts her in the hold of
a dinghy, stranded before a coyote lighthouse.

1979
Hades in Manganese

UN POCO LOCO

Bud Powell's story is never complete.
The image of a man playing blues
who earlier that day

sipped lunch on all fours
is rudimentary turning, crawling
chorus after chorus, lifting I Covers,

to view simmering Waterfront splinters,
he is visiting fist shacks,
the sipped milk becomes a dug root,

he bites into the horizon
wearing keyboard braces, he winds within
the steel cord all

who have pulled through mother recall
as the bastard spirit beyond her strength.

1979
Hades in Manganese

THE AURIGNACIANS HAVE THE FLOOR

for Gary Snyder

Now I subtract myself from the industrial
white hive, a worker slinking off
from my queen valve position,

letting it spurt, knowing that in a moment
another will be plugged in my place.
It is Soweto miners whose 115 degree eyes

gleam from the neighboring houseside,
the studs supporting our king-sized bed.
I subtract myself while I add up

the multiplication that I am part of,
the scorpion-tail cornucopia that,
with nature disappearing, the earth is becoming.

A white American male, I am already on
one of its gyroscope grooves, zooming
the inner freeway of its outer wheel.

No, I will move instead into an ancient
squad at the cenote's edge,
having concocted a message for

the Aurignacian assembly.
What does not follow is
as valuable as what does

and now what does not follow
is turning away from us.
The clawless Cameroon otter, her entire

range endangered, waddles off
dragging a chunk of MacDonald arch
while Sammy Davis Jr. continues to yell

from the other side of the Beverly Hills
tea cup we both inhabit, "Hey,
how 'bout a blanket for my piranhas!"

I feed the same peons into the same
meatgrinder that turns out groceries
for me, goldfish for Sammy's piranhas.

It is useless at last to complain about the world
all people make for each other.
Everything is owed to everyone,

nothing is owed to anyone,
a lot is owed to most
and something awful is due

to the streak of domination that somehow
does not become endangered in Shah
or peasant—sure, I know there is

a difference, but that otter would not agree
and it is that otter I am concerned about today,
wondering what she remembers

as she passes, as a species,
out of existence. I wonder if she passes
through the Aurignacian assembly,

I'd like to hear the speeches
as she presents the ogre intelligence
of her tiny arms where sounds are joisted

with water rustle, presenting the black stump
smoldering in this "new wilderness."
It is time to let the Aurignacians have

the floor, even though we suspect that
the cup shapes in Neanderthal burial slabs
are a fungus suggestion, that in death

a stem continues to stalagmite,
seeping through the crack of subliminal
scanning. I step back from this stump

onto the loosened knot of paths upon paths,
bundled by the Buddha's vatic
Gaboon viper nature. My senses must flee

to the highest bison hump. There,
a fool riding a mountain,

playing my cowpie accordion, out of which

Hades' psilocybin hair is sprouting,
while my testicles press against
what still confirms infinity,

I will accept the Aurignacian motion
that the abyss is engravable
and terminates in caves manifesting

hominid separation. I dead is under
I do, lobster verb to lobster verb.
My vertical stand on my zero.

It is now possible to chip at the target's
dead center, that bison outline
by whose manganese side I am painting

the clawless Cameroon otter
with the disappearing silver of a Dracula
stake.

1979
Hades in Manganese

PERMANENT SHADOW

There is no connection between the death
camps and Lascaux. But what if the souls

of the living dead have been tortured to
the extent that no other abode could contain them

other than that cul-de-sac that by its manganese
ceases merely to be stone hiding, but turns

in the very word *abattoir,* felling or
hide of the cave, its fell, herd pouring across

a wall turned hide, the bridge I imagine
those hunters constructed from the seal of

themselves to the animals through which
they were boring—these phrases keep backing

into themselves, as if our condition now is
hugely umbilical, a gorged boa is our passageway,

something it has swallowed whole is the messenger
between the invisible and the visibly

cannibalistic, as if the cap of Hades is
a skull drinking bowl, and the brains I mouth

and the marrow I emphasize, that which seems
central within the rings, the trident within

Poseidon, the Jupiter within light, are contaminated
by the indigestible, this fish-hook I cannot metabolize.

1979
Hades in Manganese

Our Lady of the Caves
dressed in rock,
vulviform, folded back
upon Herself, a turn in the cave,
at Abri Cellier
an arch gouged in a slab
makes an entrance and
an exit, She is a hole,
yet rock, impenetrable,
the impact point of the enigma
"no one has lifted her veil,"
the impact point of the enigma
yet rock, impenetrable,
an exit, She is a hole,
makes an entrance and
an arch gouged in a slab
at Abri Cellier
upon Herself, a turn in the cave,
vulviform, folded back
dressed in rock,
Our Lady of the Caves

As She folds back
I sense a long sentence dissolving within itself
and when it ends, it is just beginning,
a presentiment that Her sign is one turn, uni-
verse, end of a first line, curved about
a vaginal gouge, as if what is bent about is foetal,
as if She is a foetal arch bent about a slit
that goes in one-quarter inch.
Our Lady may be the invisible archwork
through which all things
shift gears in the dark, at cheetah-speed,
at snail-struggle, on the shores of Russia
where Paleo-archetypes compressed into radar
gaze around with dinosaur certainty.

Before Okeanos, continuing through
Okeanos, before the uroboros, continuing in it,
Her gibbous half-circle tells me that She was,
before an association was made between fucking and birth,

before a bubbling parthenogenesis was enclosed—
but to what extent She is
in self-enclosure, in my beak triumphantly
raising my penis to the sun,
to what extent She neatly
slides Her slit between my self and its point,
I do not know.

For the self has grown enormous,
I look through literal eyes to see Her
on a slab chopped out of Abri Cellier,
in a cool limestone room in Les Eyzies.
She seems only several inches tall.
It is a funeral to be there,
in a burial chamber where first otherness
is displayed behind a rope, with written instructions
which only describe the age of a shape.
And I who look upon this am immense,
encrusted with all my own undelivered selves,
my skeletal papoose rack through which my mother's
85 mile long legs are dangling, out of which my father's
right arm with a seemingly infinite switch trails
down the museum road, across France, to disappear
in the Atlantic, and I jig around a bit
because this ghost dance starts up as I stare
through the hermaphroditic
circle the snake made, so self-contained,
but what it and I contain, the "divine couple,"
is the latent mother-father who
has taken over the world.

Our Lady moved about
like a stubby pitchfork,
yellow fiber gushed out from between Her prongs,
She hobbled toward image—
what lurked under Her vulviform was the trident
yet to come, for men realized that not only
could the point of Her slit be hurled
but that its two bounding lines could be too,
the whole woman could be thrown into the animal.
And way in, trident-deep in Le Portel,
did Her three prongs close?
Was the uroboros hammered shut when those hunters
at last hacked themselves free from animal sinew?
And was this the point at which
the wilderness was mentally enwalled,

serpent the outer circumference,
to teach, and banish, our Adamic Eve?

Below Our Lady, on the wall of my mind,
is the foot long rock phallus Her devotees may
have taken inside while they chipped in Her sign.
I have been straddling, all poem long, that insistent,
rapacious thing, of phallus, the tooth-phallus,
the borer, for the tooth-phallus is insatiable,
male hunger to connect at any price,
but not to connect, to cease being an island,
a speck before the emancipatory shape of
the birth-giving mainland, to build a mole
to tie fucking to birth, to cease being ticks
on the heaving pelt of this earth, to hook
their erections to the sleigh of a howling starveling.
And they did
get across, at around 10,000 BC,
one night fucking and birth were connected by a mole
burrowing right under the surface of a full moon
boring a red mortal line from the edge
to a point equidistant from the circumference.
The corpus callosum was suddenly filled with traffic.
The last Magdelenians were aware that Our Lady
had closed. They padlocked Her
with the uroboros and planted the key.

She now grows on a long handle
out of ground at the edge of the abyss.
Some see Her as fly-eyed radar.
Others feel it is to Her prong that they cling
as the gale of monoculture whips them horizontal.
Many more on their knees inch along cathedral pavement
toward what they believe is her virginal compassion
which will somehow make their manure-colored
barriada water pure, their nipple blood,
their inside-of-their-bodies
muscatel in which their children play,
miracle and misery on which my index
touches, to stir for a moment Her
gouged rock socket
octopus current of
faceless suckers Veil.

1980
Hades in Manganese

THE DEATH OF BILL EVANS

Three inch caramel-colored field slug
on its back, vibrating
by the scraps of a big *Amanita Muscaria.*

It has eaten more than its size
and now its true size in visionary trance
makes me sad of my size—

I can never eat enough of a higher order
to trick the interior leper to the door,
banish him—but what would remain if I were to become pure?

Can't see the wound for the scars,
a small boy composed of scabs is staring into
the corner of his anatomy—where walls and floor end
he figures he ends, so he wears his end
like glasses before his eyes,
beckoned into the snow he will be beaten
by children he thought were his friends,
the implication of his hurt is so dark
it will scab over to be rescabbed the next time,
and he will grow not by an internal urge to mature
but by scabbings until, grown big, he will be the size of an adult
and his face will look like a pebbly gourd.
He will stay inside the little house I have built for him, in which to
    stand he must stoop.

The death of Bill Evans
makes me ask: what tortured him so?
Why did a man capable of astonishingly beautiful piano playing
    feed his leper hero-wine?
Or is the leper an excuse to modulate suffering just enough to keep
one's warmth and danger at exactly the right odds?

Eat Amanita-filled slug, I hear my death angel say,
put into yourself living poison in order to know the taste of a wound
that is bottomless, thus pure, and because pure, receptive to infection,
once infected, open to purity, endlessly draining both,
a wound in which you live like a slob and like a king,
in which you hurt yourself because you really don't care,
in which you care so much that you can't always keep caring,

so you say Fuck it
and the gourd-faced leper, misinterpreting his rot
for Dionysian exuberance, seems to drink
or makes a certain sucking motion with the mouth area of his head.

1980
Fracture

THE LOADED SLEEVE OF HADES

There is in you someone
who does not care about anyone,
whose anteater head vacuums about in the night
ingesting whatever ideology
is thrust up its labyrinthine nose—
this someone must be over 100,000 years old,
for Neanderthal began to care
strewing his dead with bachelor's-button,
hollyhock and grape hyacinth.
And did you know that caves are warehouses
in which ghosts of winds that first
investigated Pre-Cambrian earth
are also stored, so that Les Trois Frères,
coiled in tattooed splendor,
molecularly licking, still today,
its Paleolithic wounds, is affectionate,
exuberant and lethal all at once—
there is, thus, through you,
a tunnel that winds back into total discontinuity
which you tried to conceal
with the innocence that taking on the underworld
would not have repercussions.

You find yourself, at last,
as if it were a blessing, blocked by nature,
as a new plan is blocked out,
attacked by a cave
because you got too close to the Hades-Dionysus
hinged appetite. Once crushed off the stem,
Dionysus runs Hades' empty sleeve,
you might say: they join sleeves to become
one loaded sleeve, a tunnel
in which death as exuberance twisted
your ankle enough to send, once back in the car,
a cramp up into your pressed
to the floorboard spasm-rigid foot and calf.

Your fracture is a fleck
amidst global enigmatic fractions,
it is nothing and it is a headlight
frozen in a ditch, and the depth of your life?

Nothing if severed from the life of a man in rags
going off into the dark of Siberian cold.

This life that you experience as a once,
as if it were a very fine thread
disappearing into mist at both ends . . .
suppose it were dotted at both ends,
slightly beyond what you can see,
suppose the dots led off to other threads
and that you are perforatedly connected
vastly beyond what you experience . . .
suppose at this point I qualify the metaphor
so that you do not think that you are merely
spun out of something that lives off you
(*though this may possibly be true*),
and imagine your origins as that which also
travels through you, so that you are both
result and process—and if you lived
having died
while dying, could that modulate,
even control a bit, this man-damned soul-making?
Is it because you look into the mist at both ends,
certain that they represent birth and death,
that you forget so much?
That forgetting itself is a mist
in which your secrecy proliferates,
intoxicated by the thrill that comes from feeling cut off, omnipotent,
    and immaculate?

Seeing how close you came to Never
you might draw Always a bit closer,
and beg it not hide its head under its cloak—
coaxed out, would its face be hairy, yes,
and pillar-like, it would be before image,
unlike Never, which is beyond image,
a faceless face. Always
curls up under Never's tail
and manages to nurse, sending up its aniline
rodent tongue into Never's pouch of stories,
there it fishes about, like a word
inside its etymological compost.

And so the poem that is pure desire
for poem begins to accumulate—
in desire's womb there is only expectancy
for face and fingers to pry at cervix,

it is too much, this creature will say,
to live outside desire, and so
through the entire Pleistocene toward you
I have crawled, that desire can
again be world birth death dense.
And exactly what have you crawled to, desire,
your desire was wondering . . .
but now that there is no light anywhere
but no total dark either,
the hospital room fans out and out across itself
and like a fan contracts,
so that you are closed and opened
in the multiple ambivalence of your fracture,
and no resolution is sincere.

1980
Fracture

FRACTURE

The crutch you hand to another
is a furious indescribable beast,
tectiform of your own shape as Eve staggers

out of Eden, the vile legacy in hand,
wandering the dust, offering to whoever
passes a rotting piece of it, one peso,

by a Mexican roadside, her palm outstretched —
an open heart ceremony announcing
that all dark, all light, is the sawing

of being on being, a circular coring,
a ceremony lit by tapers made of entire
kingdoms. Earth, pieta. And as the dark

is serrated by the light you will start to hear,
as if at Gargas, the chalky cries of
hands, mutilated negatives, clouds of mouths

rising up the walls, virgin moths
mourning over caterpillars they have gathered
into their wings, crying the oldest cry,

that earth is responsible for our deaths,
that if we die collectively
we will take the earth with us *if we can* —

who does not hear our cries
seeks to contain us in that American cottage
where a nameless stand-in coils about

the solitary fang of a Snow White dead at 27.
Please let our howls, so elastic with water,
become that still lake most men abhor,

out of which Excalibur rises in the grip
of a drowned living Harlow whose wavering
stench of generation is holocaust to

all who seek to destroy their need
for that gleaming nipple below whose face
enwound with coral snakes is a squid haze of stars.

1980
Fracture

MAGDALENIAN

From the waist up, she is mostly headstone
and this only intensifies my love
for what we are, something walking
with snout for groin, sniffing the fresh blue
between the cracked brown bones
that are her legs. There is no horizon
to her, no explanation, only a narrative
slash above her pelvis. Something has been taken
from her, or out of her —
all I can feel, when I place a finger
on the slash, are rows of tiny teeth
as if behind them is the paradise of
mouth and tongue. Her glory is
to have nothing behind her image.
The swipe of red across thorax
is what is left after the necklace of becoming
is removed. She is
what remains after fire
and water and earth, a hardness of the air
that keeps my softness alert to the singular
voicing, the past tense of *I speak*
she seems clenched upon in belly.

1980
Fracture

TIRESIAS DRINKING

on his hands in Hades, head into Odysseus's
ewe-blood filled trench, saw through
Hades, as if "down" into an earlier prophecy:

as Pangaea separated into Laurasia and Gondwanaland,
so were creatures to separate into animals and men.
Would the separation continuum end when men

extracted language from the beasts?
As Tiresias drank animal blood to be able to speak
in Hades, so in an earlier abyss did

hominids, becoming men, swallow skulls of blood
that animal sounds might dream in them,
and take on the shapes of men? Tiresias saw

that the etymology of magic was in maggots,
each in syllable rags, wending their way
out a bison belly's imploded cavern,

that the prophet's task is to conduct
the savagery of the grass, to register
the zeros rising from the circuits of the dead

in suspension below, mouths forever frozen at
the roller coaster's summit in wild hello.

1982
Fracture

NOTES ON A VISIT TO LE TUC D'AUDOUBERT

for Robert Bégouën

bundled by Tuc's tight jagged
   corridors, flocks of white
stone tits, their milk in long
   stone nipply drips, frozen over

   the underground Volp in which
the enormous guardian eel,
now unknown, lies coiled—

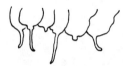

to be impressed (in-pressed?) by this
primordial "theater of cruelty"—
   by its keelhaul sorcery

      Volp mouth—the tongue of the
         river lifting one in—

to be masticated by Le Tuc d'Audoubert's
   cruel stones—
      the loom of the cave

   Up the oblique chimney by ladder to iron cleats set
in the rock face to the cathole,
on one's stomach
      to *crawl,*   working against
                  one, pinning one
as the earth   in, to, it, to
makes one   feel for an instant
feel its traction—   the dread of

               WITHERING IN
               PLACE

156

　　　　　—pinned in—
　　　　The Meat Server
　　　masticated by the broken
　　　　chariot of the earth

*

"fantastic figures"—more beast-
　　　like here than human—one
horn one ear— ⎰ one large figure
　　　　　　　⎱ one small figure

　　　　as in Lascaux?
　(the *grand* and *petit* sorcerer?)

First indications of master/
　apprentice? ("tanist" re. Graves)

t h e　g r o t e s q u e　a r c h e t y p e
_____

　　　vortex in which the emergent
　human and withdrawing animal
　　　are <u>spun</u>—

　　　　grotesque = movement

(life is grotesque when we catch
　it in quick perceptions—
at full vent—history
　shaping itself)

the turns/twists of the cave
　reinforce the image turbine—
as does the underground river,

　　　　the cave floats,
　in a sense, in several senses,
　　　　all at once,
　it rests on the river, is penetrated

by it, was originally made
by rushing water—
the cave
is *the skeleton of flood*

images on its walls
participate, thus, as torsion,
in an earlier torsion—

Here one might synthesize:
1) abstract signs
initiate movement
brought to rest in

3) naturalistic figures
(bison, horses etc)

In between, the friction, are

2) grotesque hybrids

(useful—but irrelevant to systematize forces that must have been felt as
flux, as *unplanned,* spontaneous, as were the spots/areas in caves chosen
for images—because shadowing or wall contour evoked an animal? Any
plan a coincidence—we have no right to systematize an area of experience
of which we have only shattered iceberg tips—yet it does seem that "image"
occurs at the point that a "naturalistic" horse is gouged in rock across an
"abstract" vulva already gouged there, so that the rudiments of poetry are
present at approximately 30,000 BC—

image is crossbreeding,
or the refusal to respect
the single, individuated body,
image is that point
where sight crosses sight—

to be alive as a poet is to be
in conversation with one's eyes)

What impresses at Tuc is a relationship
between river
hybrid figures
and the clay bison—

it is as if the river (the skeleton of water = the cave itself) erupts into image with the hybrid "guardians" (Breuil's guess) and is brought to rest in the terminal chamber with the two bison i.e., naturalism is a kind of rest — naturalism returns us to a continuous and predictable nature (though there is something unnatural about these two bison to be noted later) — takes us out of the discontinuity, the *transgression* (to cite Bataille's slightly too Catholic term) of the grotesque

(though the grotesque, on another level, according to Bakhtin, is deeper continuity, the association of *realms,* kingdoms, fecundation and death, degradation and praise—)

on one hand: bisons-about-to-couple
   assert the generative
   what we today take to be
   the way things are   (though with ecological pollution,
                "generation" leads to mutation,
                a new "grotesque"!)

*

to be gripped by a *womb of stone*
to be in the grip of the surge of life
imprisoned in stone
it is enough to make one *sweat one's animal*

(having left the "nuptial hall" of white stone breasts in which one can amply stand — the breasts hang in clusters right over one's head — one must then squirm vertically up the spiral chimney (or use the current iron ladder) to enter the upper level via a cathole into a corridor through which one must crawl on hands and knees — then another longish cathole through which one must crawl on one's belly, squirming through a human-sized tunnel — to a corridor through which one can walk haltingly, stooping, occasionally slithering through vertical catslits and straddling short walls) —
   if one were to film one's postures through this entire process, it might look like a St.-Vitus dance of the stages in the life of man, birth channel expulsion to old age, but without chronological order, a jumble of exaggerated and strained positions that correspondingly increase the *image pressure* in one's mind —

while in Le Tuc d'Audoubert I felt the broken horse rear in agony in the cave-like stable of Picasso's *Guernica,*
   at times I wanted to leave my feet behind, or to continue headless in the dark, my stomach desired prawn-like legs with grippers, my organs were in the way, something inside of me wanted to be
   an armored worm,
   one feeler extending out its head,

I swear I sensed the disintegration of the backbone of my mother now buried 12 years,

entangled in a cathole I felt my tongue start to press backwards, and the image force was: I wanted to *choke myself out of myself*, to give birth to my own strangulation, and then nurse my strangulation at my own useless male breasts — useless? No, for Le Tuc d'Audoubert unlocks memories that bear on a single face the expressions of both Judith and Holofernes at the moment of beheading, mingled disgust terror delight and awe, one is stimulated to desire to enter cavities within oneself where dead men can be heard talking —

in Le Tuc d'Audoubert I heard something in me whisper me to believe in God

and something else in me whispered that the command was the rasp of a 6000 year old man who wished to be venerated again —

and if what I am saying here is vague it is because both voices had to sound themselves in the bowels of this most personal and impersonal stone, in which sheets of myself felt themselves corrugated with nipples — as if the anatomy of life could be described, from this perspective, as entwisted tubes of nippled stone through which perpetual and mutual beheadings and birthings were taking place —

*

but all these fantastic images were shooed away the moment I laid eyes on the two bison sculptured out of clay leaned against what had fallen from the chamber ceiling —

the bison and their "altar" seemed to be squeezed up into view out of the swelling of the chamber floor —

the sense of *culmination* was very severe, the male about to mount the female, but clearly placed several inches behind and above her, not in contact with any part of her body, and he had no member —

if they *were* coupling, and *without* deep cracks in their clay bodies, they would have disappeared into their progeny thousands of years ago, but here they are today still, as if Michaelangelo were to have depicted God and man as not touching, but only reaching toward each other, caught in the exhaustion of a yearning for a sparking that has in fact never taken place, so that the weight of all the cisterns in the world is in that yearning, in the weight of that yearning is the real ballast in life, a ballast in which the unborn are coddled like slowly cooking eggs, unborn bison and unborn man, in the crib of a scrotum, a bone scrotum, that jailhouse of generation from which the prisoners yearn to leap onto the taffy machine-like pistons of shaping females —

it is that spot where the leap should occur that Le Tuc d'Audoubert says is VOID, and that unfilled space between two fertile poles here feels like the origin of the abyss, as if in the minds of those who shaped and placed these two bison, fertilization was pulled free, and that freedom from connection is the demon of creation haunting man and woman ever since—

we crawled on hands and knees about this scene, humbled, in single file, lower than the scene, 11 human creatures come, lamps in hand like a glowworm pilgrimage, to worship in circular crawl at one of the births of the abyss—

if I had stayed longer, if I had not with the others disappeared into the organic odors of the Montesquieu-Avantès woods, I am sure that I would have noticed, flittering out of the deep cracks in the bison clay, little winged things, image babies set free, the Odyssi before Odysseus who still wander the vaults of what we call art seeking new abysses to inscribe with the tuning forks of their wings . . .

1982
Fracture

COPROATAVISM

I rose up in the night, shat
and placed my turds, in pieces, around
my sleeping roommate's head—
then I sat on the floor, by his haloed head,
singing, "I want you to die,
Ira . . ." but he did not awake
so I rose up again, and tried to dance
like I did when I was a Scout,
hopping about him, going woowoowoowoowoo,
waahwaahwaahwaah going
way back not to a single asleep head
danced about, but to two clay bison
one about to mount the other
leaned against a rock, the ceiling is low
so when we danced around them
we really had to bend, we made some turds
out of left-over clay and tossed them
by the wall
        Diagram: 800 meters inside
   Le Tuc d'Audoubert
   rock altar
   about to couple bison
   dancing heelmarks
   turds (or phalluses)
   the wall

    There is a hole
through which I crawled,
an umbilical cord of light. I feed
in this light and it is, itself,
a tunnel, outside of which there is only
space, darkness and stars—
and a head, an enemy head that thought
me up. How I hate this head I must live by,
next to, under, how I hate having to
imagine what conceived me. But my soul, my halo material,
is stuff I have to drag out of me,
my fingers are little fangs and they tear
at the entrance of what must contain
—once the organs are pushed aside—
a chamber in which a fabulous coupling is taking place,

162

all brown, and runny, with eyes
gleaming through the powerful brown steam,
one hairy bearded dragon mounting a beardless one,
or about to mount, its pink bloody saber
braced to cleave

As the castrati hopping across the grass
Or the scribble rotting in a glass
Or the bubble opening up a cast
Or the oval opting to be round
Or the savior sitting on the ground
Or the shepherd pounding on a wall
Or Eros kicking out a chink
Or the mind believing receiving
Or Satan stoking up the alphabet
Or a sword choosing to be flesh
Or the noun humble at last
Or a cripple disturbed more than a rat

So the bison came to be married.
They were tossed like eagles, heads or tails,
still do I see them tumbling, vast hoary moths
into my kniving place—so I came to be married
to the very thing that most resists the soul,
my fecal nature, that which is speaking through me,
so do I dress my crap in white, so do I place it
carefully around my single-headed dream,
this dream that makes fun of me, that says No
when I want to crush Ira, mix Ira with

Why is the soul so brown?

Outside of nature, in sheer being,
it is very cold! To mix Ira with all the questions,
with Ire, with Why
have I moved my turds to the inner track?
Why do I no longer toss them by the wall?
Why do I dance in pajamas around this god
who will not blow me into the stars?

Cold is not the word for it, he said,
putting the last bit of shellac on our bison,
and what a crowd there will be
at the opening of the cave facsimile!
Our bison, note, never merely mine,
this measured-to-the-dent model,

this marriage of one time to another,
why, it is a marriage of earth!
To earth with hell and heaven! This marriage,
is, of
      the Earth!

    Of the green mineral water and of the bathing
    Of the keloids of the survivor
    Of the survivor grown young
    Of the spider abdomen now his belly
    Of the mantis legs now his arms
    Of the time   Of the bodies

in time.   in bodies.

1980
Fracture

VISIONS OF THE FATHERS OF LASCAUX

"The animalhood has begun to slip
we can no longer trust
the still warm tunnels of gall and intestinal
astrology in which we have failed to find
the oxygen stone but have tasted
the lees of our own trial to breathe
and there as if by telescopic
arrogance have spotted pools of dark fur
recompense for our hairless
clutching this staked out woman in whose
bloated fortress apes pass
telegrams from Africa
that a division has befallen creature"

In amassed imagination Atlementheneira
Kashkaniraqmi and Savolathersilonighcock swayed
on only one archetypal core,
intelligence had not yet been hacked from dream
dream from the frothing of the spitted kill
nor death from whole
villages of the dead living in nearby slabyards

The Fathers of Lascaux took a semen count
and found that the bison concentration
was weakening every several thousand years

Time was a lock-out each wore around his heart
a briar cage puncturing the pumping
pregnancy of shit and newborn squalling

"For I see through your eyes
thus more narrowly Atlementheneira
a star landing on an egg
and many roaches bearing crosses of an endurance beyond ours —
I fear joined with you a frailty
our skins cannot contain
the plant-eating bears nor this sky at dusk
swimming with headless starlings
and these solid fingers of weather-raked ice
jellied with water unsure of our density —

we are contracting into genital cribs
where spiders wrapped in frost curtains are sewing our bladders to
    our eyes—
what salt will remove this ravine studded with maples
what abattoir thick with Neanderthal ochre
will convert the unnamable, freeing us from the whack of navels
and the wrench of seasonal amplitude?"

So they sang their visions speech-tied
through six-legged separateness,
imbibing the fresh nasal sinew of flowers
which so stirred them that they manganesed
the terrifying gaps in the natural patchwork
subordinating the bestial slippage to vague groiny faces
and when they scrambled a cave
they added pinches of themselves and shots of the tree-like mystery of
    anatomy
their mothers wore long tobacco-leaf gowns
eyeless ghosts crawled toward the entangled speech ribbons
in which the Fathers of Lascaux were suffixing bellings with howls
waiting for lightning or a desperate pack of earthworms to remove
    their overflesh
then plaster them back with drilled eyes
into the substance of anything needing eye shapes

From which they were retrieved by the Mothers of Lascaux
whose wombs had just been vacated
while the Fathers chanted the jelly shudder of the Mothers' massive
    generative girdle
already turbine in the cave
rotating
straining the walls
priming them with menstrual effluvia
for the boundary separations to be applied by the dreaming Fathers
    who
with their sharpened tips would continentalize
the animal looping they were losing
so as to pull the animal close in image
to pry up the floorboarding of their appetites
from the ceiling of their rage
warping a space to dream a softness for the Mothers
an egg-like void in which digested meat
could be winnowed and separated like fumes
seeping up into the lower chambers of dreams
now an actual topology aslant with this earth of peaks and wallows

The Mothers were turning in a fine hum
howling like hornets attacked by orchids,
the Fathers were prying and wrenching at their abattoir boards
Mothers and Fathers cog to cog in the first
whimpering ova of the to-be-ensouled
hyena language lab of a hollow oak
there to dig out a place to live in the purple cushions of fresh-killed
    language
which had hung like bulldog saliva from their nightly fire lit lips

The separations taking place in the chambers of dreaming were
    knotted
and the tassels were swinging like sledgehammers into morning
breaking the icy light of the flat
riverine limestone into clackclack
informing them that the deadend of being born could be briefly
    tapped
that the prisoner on the other side would tap back
thus a wall, the skull clacked, separates you
from the other who is unorganized
slime and must be dreamed into erection,
as you press back in all I am will sprout
souls of lower forms, foetal shrimps coiled
about their notochords will harmonize
your desire, and the penis sentry will glimpse
the prisoner condition, big-eyed curled frog bug
do not hold back the offering
but jet it gently in this cold world
with only a thigh in the dark to lead you back upon yourself

Then the Fathers lowered the skull into the Mothers' pelvic endless
modifying corridors branching tendrils too
tight to be plumbed their bodies
turbines within rock sheath expanding against
the Pleistocene condition to burst the sexual grip
into phantoms of dreamable schist,
to fall upward reversing the animal gravity
that in icy hives of thousands of years
they had taken on forgetting the fluid
unseparated elements their pineals had steered
their sleek marine shapes through
before cosmic desiccation established
opposition, dry versus wet
the source of being yes and the source of
these Fathers' and Mothers' despair

For the pineal was now a pine cone and I
already a language orphan
and the Mothers of Lascaux flayed the penises of the Fathers
holding the rainbowed strips up into the sun
scanning them for the source of the Fathers' brutal intrusions
goring about
upsetting the glandular arrangements of seasonal rutting
treading the furrows the very day after they were reaped
pressing in again and again to contact the substance of the foetus's
    dream
in which creation was a boundless
bowling alley of simultaneous strikes and unflinching pins,
wind coiling through the blush of a dragon language rocky vaporous
    fibrous

Atlementheneira dips me into the vat of all that's gone before,
now a vanilla tar bubbling with elfcasts of civilizations,
toga-entwined axles, a passionate cobweb of liquid smiles
howling as millions of sleepers run into the rum of daylight
mixed with papyrus and rain-haunted vegetation—
and then I am out again on this German autobahn watching his
    terrible
shoulders huge as a pine forest disappear like vapor into the violet
    rainy air

The Fathers staked out a woman in Lascaux
she was their first lab, first
architecture, spread in labor,
tectiform in anatomical churn
a kind of windmill in the cave's recesses
with stretched crimson staves humming through the bobbins in their
    heads,
whose womb thus unfolded
jerked with millions of oospheric stars—
in accordance with the (now) natural law of opposition
the tube of rejection and reception had split
to ease the foetus from having to ford the atavistic Styx
clogged with the dark green fiber of monkey suicides
immense catastrophes in which hordes were snuffed by cosmic pauses
the stars went out
a blue fissure opened the earth to make it new
yes but at what loss of species thus
increased impaction in the forming world soul

This was the foetal keyboard on which each movement
depressed tones of other times

wells of disappearance Atlementheneira
was translated from a sound heard in dream
to the faint lines of a hominid atl-atl carrier
whose spear was dream
whose object was to pierce
the bloated yet severely malnutritioned
sexual bellows
releasing numbed energies to make stone
sweat red or receive umbilical finger-painted drools
as if the vagicanals had contracted the disease of consciousness
and the Fathers of Lascaux delighted entering fully
not only sentry but
the whole battalion of their wishes, winged
wishes, palaces of winged lions
crowded into the chrysalis leading to a biological
nowhere now in torque
with the Mothers to this frightening world we inhabit
in which the placental unimagined pieces
amalgamate into radar
nuclear fission the helmeted ant of dream
red visor drawn down an inch
from the twisting dreamer who still
flinches in nightmare with the rotation of

What might I offer these Fathers and Mothers?
What might I bring from the 20th century
into the humming den of their evolution to imagination,
striking out "prehistory"
dynamiting the blocked Greek passageway
so that their wet torsion smokes about
the ghastly beautiful statues of human gods
with hounds and vixens fawning about their cothurni

Suppose I placed my *Baby's Book of Events* in a niche in one of
    Lascaux's galleries
would these Mothers make anything of "Bok *Old* Mamma Tak-a *New*
    Mamma"
my first sentence in combustion with the Hitlerian Age
1937 and blood was already gushing from
the breast-severed Nanking of World Individualism
Stalin was crouched O Goya your Saturn!
my language shat in its stall
terrified stag by waterhole as the Fathers fixed
the potential to dream and scrawl the clouds of animality as they
    shredded
to open a blue immensity as if the sky

were entrance of an earth cave we were always
on the verge of leaving and so we remain
thresheld in gravity even though
the autonomous animal gods are departing
in sobbing pairs over the horizon
we grip and slide about, beginner skaters still

How would my portrait look set in a niche by an 18 foot aurochs?
Would the diffuse dread in my playful eyes
communicate even a bit of porridge to the loose electrical power lines
    in the eyes of Lascaux's Fathers?
My eyes' opposition is pyramided
with the Aztec shuttle, the Presbyterian sallow
ivorying of the groin and Dachau blow-ups.
Were the Fathers in their brutal clarities aware
that in the lifting zepplin of dream
were gases whose molecules when burgeoned
would sabotage the world tree?

I offer this entire century to these crouched tectiformers,
its crystal bubbles in which snow flurries
almost obscure the tiny stone cottage
in which the minute treasure is a hammered tongue rocking
with the verbal crib matter curled asleep in its own life,
its Hershey bar napalm license plates
bone jutting nudity dumps
Raoul "baby Incan" Hausmann
Lorca in 1928 knickers with plaid kneesox amazed
that "the most important figure in America,
Mickey Mouse," was bulldozing Catholic stonework
to erect his yellow dot sofas and draw
revolutionary whiskers on slob Latins
O pointless list, gifts for those we've wronged, all we've made
redundant before these aurochs sheaths
in which the spears of testing death
turned and turned beyond the features of mortality,
gouging off against senseless suspect stone—
the limits of yielding were made to hold
lust to penetrate Atlementheneira
was penetration itself as he hammered infantwise
against the Mother-primed tunnels
to open omen-encysted nature,
the goiter that might contain the oxygen stone,
draught of its cool burning leaves cooking
to rewind the millwheel of seasonal
green Savolathersilonighcock

gouged at a bison outline to eat
away the autumnal aromatic logic and release
in oxygen more enduring than rapture
the just beginning to dream thus omen projecting
synthesis we despair over, the human mind

As Kashkaniraqmi watching the stars
marveled at stags rhinos mammoths drifting on the same fraying
    umbilicus
so did he dream of today's Czech
pensioner in Prague by dim formica table trying to spot
the line to X for dumplings and broth—
an increasingly tendrilled fissure,
dry versus wet developed in oppositional power
to drive a slow pyramid upward in hominid constitution,
that as natural faculties weakened
armaments and medicine would increase
until men would slither like tapeworms
through button-measled gears of earth stripped to its gyroscope
    rudiments

At the base of this pyramid
the King of Cracked Morning slept
lifting his loaded sleeve occasionally
to direct the orchestration of slaves
mounting peak after peak thinking
as they struggle across solar plains they are building cities.
Evil increases relative to the steepness of the pyramid,
its latest peak is now at our throats,
as we gaze down the steps of any ruin
it is only Kashkaniraqmi who casts an archeological veil across the
    steps
to hide the bloody chewed-out teeth
the stains of dark blue amputated limbs
mossed with gangrene that cover each ascent

Around the pyramid's landing-deck
a neat atoll-like ring of smoke
resembling a tropic isle—there we live, colonial to
the subdued matted loam of wreckage
I cannot bore back to
the howl-shaped word flames of violet and blue ice that assembles
    now
a floating wall at this pyramid's tip

I would eat through this metallic smog-flavored cube
not back to some far-fetched purity or chaos
but into the heaving nucleus of femur set in bear skull socket burials
words inserted through the openings of a resistance
strong enough to hold this poem in place
even though the prisoner within the prisoner is the colonial target of
   ring
upon narrowing ring to
the strong central suck of a pupil
frosted, still alive
which I float into,
more into cooked marrow than into the language rubble of a bison
   staring,
more like ice skating in a vertical hoop surrounding me
than spitting out the hot Rimbaud rocks
to suck on cool seamless pebbles
anonymously wept for centuries in the shore coffer
of this beautiful desire to put my tongue
into the concave tongue of this Aztec landing deck,
undersea crypt where gods born slaughtered are aging

Poem, go for the throat of this crypt,
tear open a passage down to the snoring director
whose white-gloved nonhand
motions left versus right, some to torture, some to work
as the oppositional fandango increases Atlementheneira
succeeds in rubbing a black dot
against Lascaux's peritoneum, goading the cave to expel him like
   cannon shot
again he strives back against a wind tunnel of rear-wall bafflement

Why should he try to adorn stone with the cut hands and hearts of
   the moon
when the Mothers were shouting
"Don't you realize, dear one, that you wear the solar tiara? Leave
   that dark
yo yo waah waah no no ju ju ca ca wee wee
for the crossed femurs of thy rightful bear crown!"

And other Fathers than I name joined in
chanting to install the invalid personality
in Atlementheneira's antlers, to knot in his long ragged black mane
the beads of self-succession, bending him
inward against his attempt to transform the astrology of his kidneys

172

A new opposition, that he was to become his opposite
and once fixed in the Iron Maiden of self-sufficiency
to tear that selfhood off like plaster cast
yet always to reflect its scar,
the dream of wholeness rent
he limped now matured by compassion for vastly stronger
vastly more crippled nature,
he worked the vale of nature contra naturam
handling my mother rattles like liquid silver
relishing my infant eyes like oysters in the orchidwork of the night
redirecting branches that centuries later would grail about the bed of
      Ulysses,
in his manganese vale Atlementheneira could make out
the notochord of the Charlie Parker seafarer,
his ax, his quiver of blues, the dragon snout of his Melanesian canoe
he watched Bird adjust the aerial on his penis sheath
so that the lower grotesque body could contact in emergency
the geographical fixations of the mind

And as he strove against the cave Atlementheneira could envision that
      once signed
it would be relegated by gradually peaking individuality to the lower
      body,
placed in its baths, a *grottesca* of animal human copulation
Thus much of the lower body remains occult,
feces occult, semen ocult, the Muladhara Bridge
on which Antonin Artaud was sodomized by the Catholic God of
      France
as well as the internal brown phallus with its scarlet vaginal keyboard
in contact with the Mothers of Lascaux
as they wash out the Fathers on brook rocks beating
their weariness from their muscles to send them back at nightfall
into Lascaux's equine enraged crevices

The internal phallus is a spiral void chimney
leading out of the tarry baths
where urine and menses are traded on an ever bull market —
on this board are encoded the disasters of 30,000 years
there are only chipped cup shapes
before the first riverine vulvas began to meander
Entrance and Exit, a simple labyrinth,
before the Mothers and Fathers began to padlock friction
and labyrinth became complex
terminating in uroboros when the Fathers peaked
into Narcissus, recognizing
the seminal night deposit as the only wealth in a passive vault

And as the Mothers sexualized the cave the Fathers grew colder
an erectectomy had to be performed
Savolathersilonighcock was trepanned
he lay like young Black Elk nine days
then the Fathers sucked his brains
tasting the visionary prisoner raised from the lower body to a skull-
    enwalled garden —
adders flickering from their ears, they heard cock
separate from Savolathersilonighcock
the wall was language, it was the truth
but the truth had to be spread as skin, as target,
the Fathers had to spot the cave shapes that suggested an animal in
    absence
then to bore into the word itself against the mainspring now so
    sexualized
that a vortex was created to the present,
roots fracturing Ankor Vat are ghosts of these creepers ensouling
    Lascaux
the shapeshifter bristling with zodiacal light
to flood the Fathers with a desire for pelts, for animal pregnancy
so that Atlementheneira fucked Kashkaniraqmi to become pregnant
    with an ibex
and to reanimate scattered Savolathersilonighcock
forced rude gartersnakes up several of the Mothers' cunts

Several thousand years of rest for the wily Lascaux
but birthless labor for the woman staked in the shapeshifting recesses
Atlementheneira gave birth to a pawed worm
the Mothers screamed as gartersnakes bit into their simian memories
and the inheritance sacs of their minds filled with blood
the moon appeared large as a rainbow and as close, yolk-like,
flooding the tundra with pure white shadow
but the Fathers bit into the ca ca enwalled
yo treed waah waah turning no into ju ju
drawing with ju ju a cayoweeno-shaped plot
there was no nugget no reef
there was only maggot sentry-tread planted meaning
by which Lascaux was fastened to the Fathers' writhing heads
and the bison fortress with its phallus rudder removed

Relieved only by the light of milk left in male nipples
Kashkaniraqmi handled the birth clamps
minnows were used to suture the now gaping hole in the hominid
    headdress
Atlementheneira was frozen trepanning an erection
from his head to animate a natural mare-shaped contour

174

The Paleolithic delivery was under way

By firelight the verbal hydras were pathed and bound
Lascaux belched forth voids with the stench of the now profoundly
    disturbed
animal bodies which were drawn up like buckets of terrified water
Image was word pulled so thin nature
pressed its face against the tension—
many times the word broke
before its dragon contour was boundaried and wrestled onto Lascaux's
    calcite
the staked woman was worn as headgear
a trellis from the forehead to the wall was mentalized
yet to a spectator Atlementheneira
would have appeared a boy, elderly, possessed, scraggly grey hair,
    sapphire eyes,
patiently daubing red dots into a bison
to commemorate the first verbal punctures and
the joyous retreat of the rainbow moon—
his shaking arm, abandoned by the hunters,
was marionetted by the skull of intercourse
which descended by the sun's tarry ropes,
a daddy-longlegs releasing and confining
the daubed topology of bridging worlds
first pried clear in blots of fantasy
triggered by ghosts of sensations which shouldered through the
    Fathers of Lascaux
thousands of years before they became the Fathers
"It is time to withdraw the stakes from her whom we have spread
in the fantasy of an anatomical solution,"
Kashkaniraqmi saw, "and to peg down Lascaux himself
for his organs are now filled with sea water
his tentacular corridors are sufficiently fatigued from our lath-work—
we must still break his beak and puncture his bag of fluid blackness
for we are doomed to work parallel to
the ancient wet dry opposition
removing the living octopus from Lascaux's purring chambers.
Once we have established image as groundswell
Lascaux will be fixed at a calcite, mineral level—moist
yet hardened, impacted with the terror of our labor
yet airy, penetrable, a cold reserve held in flux by image

"Those to come will know of our transformation first in their own
    bodies—
when sexual reserve is broken
the poison of the catastrophe we have had to harness

175

will flood into a young man's teeth
if he were to bite someone at the moment he re-experiences this
    weaning
that person would die

"Therefore we will place the skull of intercourse close by
his pillow from the time he is born
for unless he is willing to engage us in spirit
it is best to keep this archetypal cove sealed

"What we bequeath is most dangerous—
the relay station must be kept alert
or the transformation we have performed will wither
and literal archeology, in concert with sexual domination,
will build universities in which this act we have lived for,
to reconnect the animal-bereft human-to-be to an underworld
in which a dream, not his own, can continue, will be forgotten"—
and they *did* break Lascaux's beak
using it as an engraving tool
to slash their roan colorings into the tunnel seams,
with manganese and ochre dioxide
they drilled language deposits into these seams
latticing speech to handsome mustard stallions and
the rumps of whirling ponies,
recalling the simian snake terror in mottled boa patterns
which thousands of years before
had been blisters suffered by the priming Mothers

This was the dream in which the pillars of night were to support
the dreamer's knees as he bent to drink from his hands images
that are fluid as chill air,
invisible among the morning's goldenrod
yet stony saliva foliage for the dreamer wandering
the revolving topology of ambushes he pierces
pouches of kangaroo baptism
castles enwebbed with bison cauls
razor vales ending in tusk-thatched encounters
carved artfully by the Fathers of bald grandmother Lascaux drifting
as if on leash to her furred mate,
the octopus land father, they waver
now these very very old ones as the Motherfathers
curled at 15,000 *After Image* in the human peritoneum
chant softly through mambas through constrictor doves
that all nonhuman eyes carry in miniature their flowing rock galleries
in which a crude synthesis felt sounds as the cervix neck

which when dilated revealed not only back-turned rock
fiercely possessing its molecular time
but rock they turned toward us and smoothed into aurochs flank
so that, when touched, another does not merely reflect
the catastrophic switchboard of Pleistocene day
but in that contact plants the banners of the heartless outside
by the entrance to a vision of interiority
in which covered by life
death left its mortal naming place to teach life how to pull
through faceless rock the having thundered by ancestor cavalcade
now wintered in the stall of our invaginated perdition.

1980
Fracture

A KIND OF MOISTURE ON THE WALL

Suppose earliest consciousness is worked off the shape of certain earth in-evitabilities, that the shape of Cro-Magnon "consciousness" is the contour grid of those specific caves he chose to paint and engrave.

What we call "art" may be a response to the springboard of the womb, to the shapes our minds-to-be were hit with, the tunnels of light/dark, of encroachment, of (false) release, of that move toward EXIT that one so desires, when one is governed by a crawling-ground.

The "irony" of Eden may be that exit is the organic world, the odors of wood, flower and decay that one smells with extraordinary pleasure for a few yards before emerging from a cave.

Yet Cro-Magnon, even with a short life span, was clearly not an infant. The origins of art are not squeezable baby fat, but in a Lawrencian way, are very alert to what we call "surroundings." So alert that the trap engraved in a cave wall may have nothing to do with animals but may have been an attempt to trap shadows, or hold them in place, restrain them from infiltrating the world of the living.

The first images may have been *forces put on hold.*

(for a bison with a 10-foot hump was not a buffalo; it was the Paleolithic land equivalent of the great white shark, the supreme defiance)

The bison appearing, its rump say, formed by stalactites, so that by moss lamp it is without any work by man already present in the rock wall, leads to the sensation that what is "out there" is inherent.

     *

The imagination hiding in rock lived
in concretional vaults for millenniums to be surprised
by a clump of frog-like vamps, pulsating about a pillar,
behind fuming moss, at animal parts of its shape —

they were terrified that giant elk was outside of elk,
was here, in their crawling place —
might elk be inside them?
Might all things be coming to life in all things?

They nailed imagination in place when they engraved
the rest of an elk on the basis of a rump-shaped stalactite.
But what they did not see of the elk — *was* it elk?
Or only elk rump expression on the face or body of something
showing itself momentarily in their fire,
something bigger than the cave,
something slumbering or awakening in the earth?

And the questions? A kind of moisture on the wall.
What was not there might be them.
What is clear: something was in motion that can still be seen,
as clearly today as when the first ones tried to arrest it
by completing the elk outline inside of which
the engraver scratched part of a woman's body with lances
extending from it as if they were thongs to "stitch" her body,
headless, shoulderless, to elk body, as if to decomplete
the finished outline, to question the idea of completion.

A headless shoulderless woman running filled with lances
across the rock of a tautly pinned elk is the sensation of imagination
as it pours through life like hoarfrost, or liquid jade,
the rock wall itself writhes so stilly
that something never to be completed writhes in us,
ringworm intrigues, the tentacular lava of maggot-
lined fables. The moment we touch anything
that touches us the entire human body becomes a pipeline
of inverse fire hydrants wrenching shut the feeling valves,
for to totally connect with even the stain of an image is fearsome,
a cog to cog movement in an enrapt reporter calling up
the abandoned elevators of the lower simian body
derailed in Africa millenniums before, those rotting luncheonettes
visited only by hyenas and ferocious striped worms,
those bleached cabooses individuation pretends
to have left behind but which lurch open onto our brains in dream
to keep us open to the future of an earth
awesome, infinite, coiled in hypnosis.

1982
Fracture

TOMB OF DONALD DUCK

for Leon Golub

I. *Apparition of the Duck*

O my white, white father, you were the bell
dong clapper and tower of a construction arisen
from the "Aztecland" of an Indian's hump burst
like a boil into the savage clanging he must wear
like a headdress of fruit

and because I too am white, does my word xerox
its tongue to become
a pool of blood and green oil
out of which a dead ermine is lifted
and rung out in the sky over Beverly Hills?

Tumblers of a safe in this sky
from which drip peelings of a billion comics,
the feathers from your sexless bottom Uncle Donald
drift south to
children who run to the potless source of this rainbow sortilege,
a male parthenogenesis sprung from
an Olmec-sized Disney head

(my speech on behalf of the wretched
is screened by my North American whiteness,
glass enclosure in which an actor
wrings from his hands special effects
which need only be wound up to be heard again)

No change no growth no death no past
no animals
with fake animals for pets
the body a highway of zippers smooth metal interlockings

What is in the Junior Woodchuck Manual of your tomb, Donald?
A needle slipped into a child reader's fantasy
injecting adult anxieties
into his neotony.

II. *Toddler Under Glass*

There was no time until the first word sirloin was sliced
this sirloin was dite (light)
chur (picture) cock (clock)
and the speaking? Two dis-
combobulated rug cutters, speech
crossing and crossbreeding not
as in Surrealism but as in Paleojitterbug
where speaking is by extension midden
by extension mam-a
growth by apposition
"the deposition of formative material in successive
layers" wa-wa (water) chup-chup (bird)
O yellow po-ca dicka-da of an owl yet to be conceived
even before the egg
I've been betrayed by the earliest star
and by the horsies on my pillowcase
by pillbox mother by pillbox father
fortifying themselves as words begin to form
whose kisses are firing
and to fire is to leave a rapture that is sheer jingle bells
"What don't you do anymore?"
within days of being shown the Bible, specifically Don't
Grunt Panties, Chapter 4, paragraph 34,
the wedding of Donald and Daisy, or
the collapse of Isaiah, the rubber auto Isaiah from Elkhart —
outer darkness suddenly filled with held-back erections
all aimed at 2035 North Meridian Street
going off as I bounce in your lap
happier to be here than anyplace else in the world
Whose world Popeye wonders,
Boon-man's? And it is true:
I screwed NO into the God photographer's lens
so that, snapped, I would not reproduce my dad-da,
knead his Smokey Stover,
enfoo dern sech weather, O mutter of us all
didn't I ever tell you how it was to be two?

TODDLER UNDER GLASS

cooked but uncarved, under mam-a's firm hand
No one was going to serve *her* dream
I bunched up on my suddenly confined crawling-grounds
while relatives' faces fun-housed thanksgivingly in the glass
and her face fun-housed in my own

my very first mask on which ca-caw (Santa Claus) crawled
a language-mask heh-heh (for Sonny)
Bok *old* Mamma, tak-a *new* mamma
bite of wa-wa words
bok windmill sound child, bunched on the social platter
frightened of losing my wow-wow my ga-ga
a baby mammoth in the peekaboo
I-see-you snow mounting from below.

III. *The Severing*

In essence we do not want to be outside

yet the only way back in is through death
and the beast was the god of death
putrifying about man
not yet man but something
so cold for so long, so cold
that too much of his life was now in his eyes —
his sex had so contracted
from the misery of copulating in ice
that it expanded, a bulb in his head
sending out tendrils into his irises so that
instead of continuing to turn, helplessly,
on the winch of beast and season,
man saw, sexually, that the world was something to enter or
to withdraw from, and that his dead
were in sexual remission but would return,
smaller and not that much more trouble to take care of
than when they left, for the point of withdrawal
and the point of re-emergence were hinged,
the vulva at this time had only an exit and an entrance —
it had not yet become a maze

The mystery seemed to take place behind the vulva's centerpost,
try as he might
man could not figure out what woman did with the dead
to decrease their size and increase their howling

Seeing that he roamed the tundra
a parasite in the earth's fur,
man, in his own eyes, began to emerge,
a sort of tick in the animal *Knockwurst,*
part of it but not the same, and to feel this was first
jubilance and first sorrow, such twisting of

the feeling bones against their own sinew
that man began to paw meaningfully
inside the earth of his beasts, began to scrape
as if he were a foetus returned to the womb
having seen the world outside,
he saw that his scraping left marks,
path snarls, vulva-shaped calls,
that he recognized life in what he scratched,
and that he was a smoldering hybrid
with rock and hardon bobbing about in a tundra of congealed
blood that he could soften with his breath,
that this gelid blood, this matted glassy meat, yielded
precisely a him
twisting against its beast webbing, so he followed
labyrinthine tunnels, dancing against his own exit and entrance,
the world was uteral and urinal,
where he pissed and spat and scratched
a diorama of his condition appeared,
the outlines of the animals he scratched were his own meanders
inside of which he was a ghost on fire, something with its liver
sewn onto its face, sewn through with beast stitching,
which today, without the rest of the fabric, looks like spears

and as he chipped into the clitoral centerpost
as if to insert his own twist into his exit
he was casting off that which he had entered in order to exist
so that he was his own S sprout
in the deadness of his exit

man in slow motion shattered his beast
so that only mask bits of ears, paws and horns were left
on a shape that more and more resembled
man glaring back, in a dance hex,
glaring in heat, but in the heat of withdrawal,
to shake off the clitoral shadow of what he could not cut through.

He took his iced lust for the mystery he could not penetrate
and attached it to all the beasts,
hinged it to them as if to mirror that from which he was hinged
    away —
he masturbated animal shadow so that it bulbed and throbbed
into wings or several spitting heads or jutted human breasts
and the mystery could be fought in the name of the Fabulous Beast —
he invented Hercules and Portculis
in order to disguise his nakedness,
and as he battled with the spectres he had turned his own

enthroned placenta into, as he covered world with himself,
as he hacked up actual beasts,
he brought the underworld to its knees —
at which point it went into revolt:
the powdered bone man brayed his beasts into eventually
became Goofy and Mickey and Donald, dotted eidola
flittering about their cages in newspapers, books and films,
empowered with the wrath of a satanized underworld
set loose with the power-lines of media,
an underworld composed of all the hydras, manticores, gorgons,
lamias, basilisks and dragons, and it is from this perspective
that the shadow of every duck is shaped like Donald
and that Donald has the power to leave the duck
as hagfish are said to leave their lairs at dusk
to all night long bore into the souls of children.

IV. *Stud-Farms of Cooked Shadows*

The Rolls Royce parked in an El Salvador prison yard

Inside the car, beefy North Americans eating an elaborate picnic lunch,
delicately unfolding white cloth napkins, licking their fingers, each fingernail
a mirror reflecting a cage in the "hole" in which a living person is com-
pressed. Chicken. Cheese. And an iced Lucifer to wash down the Rolls
Royce in flames the couple inside undisturbed because the wealthy do not
burn an invisible wall of asbestos a mile thick protects even me from the
worst there is
        I sit at my desk in the glare of the prison wall observing
the car which the artist is tearing the insides out of like a living peasant
can be disemboweled with a dull knife say, you can watch his face twist
beyond noise into the pleasure on my countrymen's faces as they pack prison
yard dirt into the Rolls, the idea is to turn it into a little jungle with
sprinklers in the roof, so that in juxtaposition jungle to jungle the men
in cages can be mailed through *Time* magazine and sniffed
                              Machete blow
with the North Americans as the cutting edge strolling away like a ham-
merhead shark cruises the evening of his hunger these words pass through
the prison and you become annoyed that the color in the flowers now seems
to be affected by an "us" that is the prow of Good Ship Machete as it
wanders hungry without mouth mouthing without hunger the welts on
the nipples of a 12-year old Indian boy it is the child, Donald, I keep coming
back to as I sit in prison moonlight on the lid of your grand sarcophagus — for
years I thought I was in the crypt of the Temple of Inscriptions at Palenque
dreaming of a cannibal feast; tonight I know that I am but that the chiseled-in
king is you and that in your stunning whiteness without orifice is buried

a duckling, better a drakeling since duck is feminine meaning you've eaten the Virgin Daisy of our hearts. I lift your lid, Donald, to realize that you are a flaccid black hole, contactable only through my own lost childhood and it is terrible to watch all of you quack along exchanging wristwatches for native gold against the backdrop of the Aurignacian Summation the whole scene becomes the slitting of an Amazonal throat but I cannot make you real, Donald, I can only talk to you as Syberberg talked to his Hitler dummies as your own heil ascends from a tomb whose bottom is engnarled with the construction of the underworld itself and with my own two-year old word forming in 1937 when terror shifted gears in Europe — what shall we call these innocent adventurers decked out in comic book animal auras? Carolyn Forché said the El Salvadorians' ears in the colonel's sack looked like dried peaches and that a few which fell to the floor seemed to be pressed to the ground or listening to you and me, Donald, here, these grand reservoirs of human energy fried into ghettos in which no one could be said to live, cages in which the living are the shadows of other living — that colonel has no shadow, in all the taut suspenders of his anxiety he is content to be carried around the prison yard, like we used to play as kids, on the back of a peasant whose belly is a dugwork of running sores These sores, Ladies and Gentlemen, are only putrid at their place of origin, once the gunk is canned — since no production exists in your world, Donald — it's fucking good to eat, and even though the ride is bumpy at times even though the cries on TV seem menacingly near it's all Starsky and Hutch, isn't it, a heaving friendly world with the slaves sleeping in their own shit a few inches below the floorboards of this earth on whose back I too ride, since to blow up the Rolls is only to make it bigger to arm it more fully, so that this lunching pad for the rich, this car converted into art, this interior soul sprinkling is all taking place inside something that looks like a petrified apocalypse, weapons sticking out of every pore, with Manson in the American underworld, eating one of his Kali Krishnas whenever he gets hungry but hoping it will all be over soon so that with what is left of them he can climb back to earth and assume that role he has deserved from birth, namely to be buggered very badly at 12 so that he can look through the wet curtain shreds of his ass and stick his tongue out at this little Indian or little dummy I should say, for there is no one here, Donald, but my fingers tracing again and again the carved contours of your sarcophagus lid, like God might run his claws over the topology of Disneyland, a blind god, a creature still hovering over the primary waters, urine salt a lizard's tail and a peasant's heart mortared into a tiny soft black sun which I place in this crippled alembic knowing the irreality of my words taking place in the automagical washing machine of North America, this whirl of films watches umbrellas records Donald Duck soaps even, rocking-chairs neckties condoms? Disney as Bruckner, on his knees in the gravity-filled end of the tear of a heaven-suspended condom praying at full vent for all the little children everywhere to coalesce into nine-year old himself at dusk somewhere in Chicago, 1910, delivering his papers with nothing nothing on his mind but his most evil father flowing in the condom walls of snow as he trudges the hamster belt of an anger never to be fully expelled until, we say, what? But the world does not change, it only grows lighter and darker, lighter when darker, darker when lighter, the blue green glow of Eden down there in El Salvador turns out to be a horrifying wound operated by maggot men preparing street urchins for computerized torture under the gaze of fly men backed up by vulture men backed up by the "compassion" of the stars, and the howl of this wound is so wide that it is the sound of the very day itself, the solar day like an opened heart packed with siphons and drains, feast parked in the heart of an Indian mother whose breasts are no more than ripped lips

Sounds like an accident outside

Outside? No it is just that mother's defoliated eels pawing toward her through the pyromaniacal air.

1981
Fracture

THE LANGUAGE ORPHAN

The I,
barque docked at the doorstep of no one.
In it, an infant ages, unnursed,
at last elderly, crawls over the side,
down the cobblestones, in his weather-
stained Sweet Pea regalia . . .

There is nothing sadder than watching
what is anonymous at the heart of all
crawl in place. The street, the houses,
even the trees, are what move.

At times, in dream, you join the language orphan.
In an unfurnished moonlit avenue
you snap on his leash.

Isn't he your radar, really,
what keeps drawing home through you,
you, the unused needle,
home the infinite thread.

1982
Fracture

MAITHUNA

Caryl's delicate hand—reaching—in sleep
my side, out of which a turbulent river pours,
to sheathe her hand and arm, to cocoon,
protect her—and in doing so, lying awake
I watch her grow monstrous, a creature of my imagining—
her body wet, feathery with slime.
                        Now I am wrapping her,
as if with long silken vegetal bands, binding her
with the freedom of my side, spear place, gore
transformed into a vault of liquid thread,
spool vault in which the swastika of aggression
is dissolved by a harem of tentacles
into this magical moonlit thread—
                    so, do I hesitate
as if from fear of the labyrinth of syntax
binding you binds me into? Already only your heart
can be seen, the truffle center of a winding
that even wound tight is loose and curling,
a train of cloth draped about the rocks over which
I am crawling with you stitched to my back.

So there is no ending to the shrine
constantly fastening and unhooking, for I have seen
the husks of your eyes at night littered about the world,
still glinting with the nickel mystery of the interior,
still moist although all the flesh about them has been eaten
by "the likes of me"—is it eons ago? Or did I,
just a moment ago, convert my kissing into infantile
hunger and with all my teeth turned into penises
break up and suck in your soft, soft tofu interior?
I must have—yet you are still outside
and radiant in this after-intercourse Maithuna.

Through the translucent bindings I can see you slowly
begin to form your own world,
                      in your flipper-like hands
you hold a glass ball in which is reflected
the face of creation, for having penetrated you
I have been offered sabbath, our bed is crisscrossed
with rainbows, blood edged, with violet
interiors, the wart hogs have stopped

188

their horrible breathing, for a moment the whiskey
mattress in Alexander Haig's voice collapses,
heaps of disemboweled peasants rot into it,
and the world is fungus, with vermicular elves busily
shoveling and restoring.
                              And now as you expose me
to the hexagonal formation of hovering wasps
I receive the discharge of eggs, loading them in here,
kissing an identity to each. Miraculous conversion of my plight
from having left the mat of tusks and
the bright-red mouth of writhing hair—to move
into the image of you as through eelgrass,
to hold in outstretched hands the torn pods of your Ice Age
distant eyes, to feel the iris pulse and implode,
to watch the wart hogs take off their tusks,
empty them of powder, even unscrew their hooves
packing themselves into the lining of my wound.

1982
Fracture

THE COLOR RAKE OF TIME

I dreamed that all artists were friends,
that we told everything we knew to each other
and that our knowledge was physical,
that we worked in the skull rooms of each other's
genital enclosures, broken fulcrum people
raining within ourselves at high noon,
that we talked in mid-ocean in smashed saint stables
where spars were severe-steady cave-ins,
that at last all of us feasted off repression and depression —

I dreamed! that the sphinx was not at the end of her twig,
that she was not open to the furnace of the hearth,
that there was no heat without recall,
no vitality without memory, that the slave was merely one
who rowed in a hold without oar-lock . . .

then I heard the color rake of time
scraping the window, and awoke to the face of God
whose childhood is everlasting
whose maturity we struggle to create.

1982
Fracture

IV
ANTIPHONAL SWING

"Whispers antiphonal in azure swing."
— Hart Crane

AUTO ————

My name is Charles Bernstein
I eat his pears
and walk beside his wife,
I work the hallucinatory
triple-tipped fruit hanging from the soul of man,
his desire to rain.
I am that form of death that is self-duplicity,
I wear his pale shirt,
I know how much he loves electrolysis,
or migration velocity, the way nouns
change countries, or verbs
into spermy-tailed adverbs,
I am the double who is not him,
his double's death, or djinni
with the light brown mare,
a light-crowned phantom
I milk his pears, I wear his wife,
I work his desire for migration,
I do not know this man,
I am the spot between,
caught between Eshleman and Bernstein
a useless hoop,
the secret sharer the Doppelgänger the face in the Larwell churn,
my name is Clayton Eshleman,
therefore I disregard these pears,
I climb down my spider thread from the sparking clouds,
into the abyss, the Buddha thread,
it is a moral descent, an electric abyss,
alert as those little birds who live
on the crocodile's gums and peck lunch from his teeth,
I enjoy being a parasite on a curvilinear, reptilian bias,
because I am Charles Bernstein
I am bored with all these spermy-tailed dreams,
I have decided to exercise a between,
to give a rubberiness to nothing,
there are very special children to be found here,
beheaded legless integrities,
for there is always a thief tossing in the muck "down there"
willing to say anything to elevate his station,
my name is Charles Eshleman,
I am trying to get out of hell without the same old sad story

and as the Buddha thread descends
both spider and I become conscious of all the others
who would like to use this language,
this plot, this trauma,
this tomb in which a furious bobbin is at work.
I was born in Wakarusa, Indiana, 1891, the brother of Clayton,
ran the Eshleman Machine Shop, married Iva
my daughters are Faye and Fern, long very white plants
that spread out through underworld water,
the inner squid father, so tender I am like floating rot,
but I encyst and pervade,
I make the hit parade,
as Clay Bernstein I drove many a buggy,
I never looked at who rode in my carriage,
I think it contained a huge white snake named Emily
coiled on the velvet seat, viewing herself in a hexagonal mirror,
swollen with milk she was on her way to the underworld
to bear a very precious ink,
as origin redoubles in associative elasticity
this act of doubling is severe subtraction,
this is a voice neither Clayton nor Charles,
or either of their doubles,
I am the ghost in the square, bounded on each side by a name,
I am the hole in the symposium,
since I belong to no one I have no ego
and can assert myself, the lamp post
following Francis Bacon down Primrose Hill,
the enjoined double, the double not a double,
the adobe, the stuff that holds
the serpent's shape, an energy
caught between static flesh and
a fleeing combustion, a jewel afloat
edible lotus, the fiery letters on the rim of the Grail:
Dear Poets, Please re-establish my benevolent rule—
Eliot's *Waste Land* mainly proclaims
the failure of Western poetry to retrieve
my soul from the limbo into which
Christianity had burned, raped
and reversed me. Butchered ladies,
like Roman police photos of suicides, drift in *The Waste Land.*
You must see through its nightmare.
This poem is ruled by only one
of my damaged aspects, the fear of death
combined with a flying worm at home
in the rosary of blood, for the serpent I love lives
in blood, and not "spilled blood,"

and because I adore these things
I have no home, not even a mind to dwell in,
I'm an I drifting through light as if to fall in place on a dog,
think of me as stripped furniture, the bed of Penelope,
think of me as Ariadne, dead, but giving birth, the Minotaur my
   midwife,
think of the hominid crouching beside the dead ape
drawing forth your fuselage and mine, all our struts, our hubris,
beside the hearth after the Titans had been put to bed
and our parents, Female Stairway
and Male Hope of Treasure Below,
lost themselves at their desk, before retiring,
over the hopelessly screwed up accounts.

1983

JUNK MAIL

I have been invited to the third Creativity and Madness Conference, Easter Week 1984, at the Sheraton Royal Waikoloa. After "Pablo Picasso: The Blue, The Rose, The Cubist, THE MAGNIFICENT!!!" there will be a Singles Luncheon (Dutch Treat) followed, 4 hours later, by A Piano Concert of Chopin and Brahms by Ms. Ostwald, presumably the wife of Peter F. Ostwald MD, author of "Music and Madness: The Inner Voices of Robert Schumann," who will, just before the Singles Luncheon, have lectured on "Music, Ambivalence, and Bachelorhood." Tuesday April 17th will start off with a bang: after Bahman Sholevar's "Descent into Hell: Basic Mistrust and Ego Despair in the Poetry of Sylvia Plath and Anne Sexton," Dr. and Mrs. Carder will present "A Marital Crisis as Revealed in the Music and Art of Arnold Schoenberg." After "Charlie Chaplin: A Life Observed" there will be a Sheraton Royal Waikoloa Roundup Dinner and Show (optional). After Dr. Sholevar has displayed Dante Alighieri's Ascent to Heaven, the movie THE TEMPEST will be shown. A previous conferee commented: "*Creativity and Madness* was enjoyable in every conceivable way!"

*

The difficulty of creativity and the despair of madness have been
    dumped
into a trough called Enjoyment. *Fun* is the word, I think
for what the participants are geared for, not Maenads
raving on the endless Styx of a threadbare psyche,
nor even a scrutiny of how the thread might have disappeared in its
    appearance
to John Wieners or Diane Arbus. To place an "And" between
    creativity and madness
sets up a momentary LSD icicle in whose blade a glorious disorder
sticks out its tongue, or the not inaccurate hunch
that in creative grandeur another world is manifest, and when one
    finds oneself
wading for days in a lagoon of blood with no sun no moon but only
    a roaring as of surf
around one, one must have the candle of one's split open mind lit
or all that we seek to leave but so depend upon for meaning
is engulfed. But what could those of us who *have* had our arm
    around Nebuchadnezzar once, who
have at least been penetrated by the smell of crawling in a gibbous
    circle in a dark hut—what *can* we say

to those who would season their Royal Waikoloa Singles Luncheon
with
"George Orwell and Rudyard Kipling: Abandoning Parents and
Abusing Children?"
There is a repression in North American psyche so tough, so
uncontactable because of the depth, now,
of the suffering midden of humanity creating goods for us,
that it is no longer disturbable—it can *enjoy* ANYTHING! Can
enjoin any grief and discuss it
over pineapple—but I cannot fully believe this or I too would be
consumed. That the shirts of these people
are being made somewhere in the world where the workers live less
well than our pets
can turn the vise of the creative mind into itself to the point that not
madness
but a simpering, descriptive, situation comedy runs out,
a pseudo-art the equivalent of the lectures to be delivered there.
And how much of those doctors and their well-heeled patients are
packed
like a chamber of bullets in my own mind?
For I can actually see myself *enjoying being there.* I'd blow up 48 hours
after arrival.
But my gregarious North American nature is so social it dives into
any human pool with the drunken recklessness with which I used to
leap,
with friends, into the Bloomington quarries in utter blackness at 3 AM
knowing we'd be, if lucky, missing jagged rocks 30 feet down there
by a few feet—
I say to this nature: I know how powerful you are, how ego potent
your lust
to protect and propitiate your so-called innocence. In the soul-less
basement of this country
it is you who are at play, ceaselessly reassembling the heating system,
occasionally
braining your puppy with your little wood mallet, amazed and
delighted he springs back to life, amazed and delighted that mother
and father
are out on endless chores, daddy over Nicaragua loosing last night's
supper,
we don't know where mommy is, she may be at the market or at
choir practice
but her condition is *we don't know where she is,* so little Me looks
around
with glazed wild-eyed friendliness—maybe he should go look for her!
But when Me

looks for something, it does not go out, it only goes in to a more
 Meish aspect of itself,
it reclines on the basement floor, unzips its little pants and pulls out
 like magician's streamers
the cloth of its own hunting scenes, timeless yet timed, edged with a
 sportive fuse.
Nothing, charmed from its nickel dungeon,
eyes this little fellow like we frat rats used to eye
a frightened, unsure, slightly ugly, clearly needy girl.

1984

AN EMERGENCE

Anna Della,
  uncut block,
free of hostility and
  aggression —

I think of your face
  I've not yet seen —
I imagine it as a miniature
    of your mother's,
glowing black fringed face,
  an uncut face,
as the Taoists would say.

In the translucent submarine of your mother's arms,
flowed about by the ocean of forms.

At your age — several weeks —
I dreamed my mother was a rhinoceros, dancing hard,
stamping out a fire that hissed and struck at her.
  O, like you,

I could not say my dream, from the deep pouch of the crib,
the deep, deep elevator well of the crib,
over which, eyes — or stars,
      shaped blocks,
    stared into
      my maggot loveliness,

as I churned the tenuous
vibrato of my mother's
    and my father's milk.

Anna Della,
    unspun web
of your mind . . .

O, on her slender hind legs, she danced and danced,
O, the speckled red snakes hissed and struck at her.

  Like you,
I could not spin my dream,

pregnant with my web, of another order,

I could not protect my
        mudra mother.

The baby *was* dreaming, and this might have been her dream. Our mothers
rearing upright, dancing out, dancing against, an alien order that would
poison or swallow us, might be in our faces as with an expression that
includes all nos and yeses we surface, still womb-clad in fermentational
freshness. The dream is, then, pollen slipping off mind-stalks tilting like
reeds half in, half over, water, with the infant's tender muscular recall,
a toy-like pulley in the misfiring of so many adult signals.

                She cries and cries
until the word spider
drops a glyph of her natal daemon into the web of her dream,
and vanishes, trailing its long silvery legs, squid-like,
as if the night air
        were *under ocean,*

            unborn,
and she is
the only thing alive.

O, what does it feel like, this glyph?

                Why
to read it will it take all
your life?
            And all your life
to realize that to read it
you have dreamed away your tender muscular recall,
your mind-stalks tilting
    half in   half over
            water,
your womb-clad fermentational freshness,
the pollen of your smile?

What seems to be *the* dream turns out to be a loop in the web of the
awareness that constellates one's life.

She lies in her crib, a closed triptych,
the third day of creation sketched lightly on her face,
shores emerge, the earth puts forth pincers through an armored
    cliff . . .

deep in the displacement of the crib,
in the shaft of unelevated night,
the plasma of form, milky trolls, giving bridges over
    a pool where a platypus is doing her wash . . .
out of the pool a mind-stalk is rising, it has a single eye,
in whose globe a veldt shines, giraffes are grazing,
a fire glows uneasily, thunder, a rhinoceros mother
    rears and on legs so slender dances
hard against the snapping, hissing snakes, she would trample
    what chased us back up the trees,
gusts of Shival recall, it is as if one
unborn cried out, to protect her birthing mother
        against a viper order.

This is a charm

        against displacement
        against unelevated night

I thought of you when I rose
to make Caryl's and my supper.
We'll eat salmon steaks,
but for you —
    inspissate mother
for weeks and weeks.

1985

THE NATAL DAEMON

The navel
haven, that landing place
with a screw-shaped runway,
closed
for the season the sign might say, closed
for duration, closed duration,
minute cenote, crimped
flesh freckle into which you
will not allow
anyone,
because all the sores, the sweetnesses,
all the touching things about a person
are known there, the navel
is more than a palm or
a penis print, the navel, the
nothing indentation, nasty
little cave where all the childhood
sandbox catshit is in memory stored.

*

Navel intelligence is periscopic, and relates to and from all. What has been
written about it? The navel is the well of the mini-void entwisted in all
of us, it carries the eye of our smell, our natal other, who never leaves
us. In our navels are the remains, the archeology of our mothers' amplitude
of feelings. It may contain a dead other. Its soft, downward, inward screwing
simple folds issue the intelligence of the Ethiopian scribe, Adonolutus. It
is said that Adonolutus upon birth was plunged headwards into his own
navel where he remained for 31 years. He lived on his side, fed through
tubes in his back, and was taught to write by kindly teachers in the court
of Nectooki the Third. His collected writings only come to 84 pages but
they constitute the only body of navel intelligence that has come down to us.

*

As we are born,
something is born with us that we cannot bear.
Or are we born on the navel
anvil of a natal daemon?
As infants, do we voluntarily submit to its power?

And if we do, must we later blind this daemon to
release ourselves from its material perspective?
What this is
must be much older than "natal daemon" can symbolize—
it may be the amassed inherited weight of biological consternation,
the perils of the Ulysses-like journey of the sperm
toward the Penelope of the poised receptive body that can accept
or reject this "husband," this one who seeks to be bonded
to the house of the egg, which is a place of spinning,
of doing and undoing, a webwork whose queen
may devour as well as embrace her wayward consort,

the knot of trauma, or plot, the dream weft within
our being forced out
is a being received into,
                    a being,
whose face, like a malformed vagina,
appears on certain cave walls
                    (it has a small berry in its mouth
that it appears to be expelling and sucking in,
a portable nipple or edenic raspberry, its bubble-like
"charm" to be slid under the poet-to-be's skin
like a pebble in an untake-offable shoe)

From a Platonic perspective we are
to release ourselves,   "For this whole story relates to the descent of the
soul into this terrene body, and its wanderings and punishments till it returns
to its true country and pristine felicity."

The poet is a problem for any perspective that is linear,
evolutionary, that posits a purity, fallen from, to be returned to,
for he *cultivates* his natal daemon,
enduendes it, since in its tormenting appearances
it shakes off that venomous dew he needs
"to smoke his melons," to fertilize
images embedded with their own destruction and renewal,
complicated by the never totally-transformable presence of the daemon

The conversation of all the natal daemons in the world
—something to be heard! I suspect certain animals hear it,
like a deep gurgle of bees
in the roots of that tree, whose shaft and branchings
our groins would erupt into
had we not, so long ago,
harnessed our genitals, cursed them to become workhorses

to transport our loads of picked souls
from the palace of the cherubim to the valley of the chopped and
planted king.

1985

LEMONS

These lovely freaks, skins
pulled tight about inner disturbance,
a kind of vegetal lava—a one-eyed
face looks out of a blackened
yellow cowl, an eye held in its tensile
puckered mouth

    *

As if I held in my fist a creature
not my hand, a head on
the end of my arm, a head twisted
with wrath, whose soul spills into
the air as I ungrip

    *

Some are peaked like elves' shoes,
Aladdin slippers, as the arabesque
of cosmic charge tips
  instead of curling on
  into a seamless sphere

    *

One I know has a small aperture
with which it gently grips one's
        distended finger —
          a kind of vegetal navel,
    the suck we feel
  in the presence of lemons
no symmetry no
No

    *

I do not know what to say to the force
in the lemon tree behind the bedroom when sleepless at 3 AM
I think of the lemons as heads,
headlets with frozen howling mouths,
a tree of tiny perfumed skull-lives

*

One said: "to dangle here,
        all belly
        on the stem
        of another mind"

nun face, with so much God contracted

        navel face

could I but think with my navel
would I see each being's aura
as a palace of umbilical corridors?
        *

It is good to be on earth.
Two fresh slit lemon halves
draw my heart out of its hiding heart space
        *

Enter the mind of a lemon
the sweetness of rock
the soul of things that speak
only in the interface of us and them

                            1983

NORA JAFFE

The journey from the hand to paper,
the journey of the hand. As it inches along
a rocky grass-plentiful landscape,
a hand, clutching its debris, its pencils —
and behind the hand, the boxcars of the body,
whose length, from this perspective,
disappears into the distance where
it continues to coil out of a shell,
out of a small enclosed lagoon . . .

You were sitting in your studio, making this journey
several hundred times a day.
The miracle is that the hand's journey,
the rocks over which it crept,
its resting spots, its anxiety over the length of
the body behind it, *is* depicted,
its contact with its road, its scratches
are traces, and the body it pulls along slowly
passes through the whiteness of God
into a dimension on the other side of nature.

O the number of nights, the number of days
this hand camped out, this palmer
with its tokens. Had it visited the Holy Lagoon,
the source out of which its body had first
been dragged up on a bank and then on,
this delicate serpentine body
forever out of its element, across the rocks and brush?
The accumulation of nights and days, yes,
the long ongoing attempt to draw out and to draw
all the markings of a life so
unique and so other, so fusioned with atavistic
relief, a hand among all the hands,
crouched below its palm, a pilgrim under
annunciation, the forever returning Figure of Her
stepping down through the starry darkness,
She of the muffled white robes, flowing yet
bound, a nomad angel, furled from foot to head,
whose bindings, whiter than her limpid garb,
seemed orchestral thongs, to tie her into
the lightning-like framework, the bound woman

bound into the greater woman of the night sky,
this angel

who commanded you to bear
her convexity here, her shadow
a robed phallus cast,
the heart's sacrifice,
into the still Lagoon,
obsidian surface. Cracked
egg out of which
this palmer coiled.

And again you lean toward the tilted board,
Nora,
over *your* hand, *this* hand, *whose* hand—
as it feeds at the base of a pyramid of light.

1985

TUXEDOED GROOM ON CANVAS BRIDE

[tuxedo. From the name of a country club at Tuxedo
Park, near Tuxedo Lake, NY., fr. Lenape *p'tuksit,*
an esoteric term for wolf, lit., he has a round foot,
the name of the Wolf subtribe of the Delewares.]

The artist in tuxedo with cigarette instead of brush,
in undertaker clothing, with surgeon white beneath.
His body in the black sleeves of a repressed
belch, staring, at what is behind his eyes:
gas from the social wafer,
the one with manhole lids and cathedral flagstone.

Max Beckmann had round feet and was a wolfman as he tore
his tux into shred-like spars to keep afloat
through two World Wars — bandages to bind
the "infinite divinity" of God to "arrogance before
God, defiance of God, because
he has created us so we cannot love ourselves."

A black impasto to deaden the edges of human bodies,
to scab pores so that the bestial God would suffocate,
so that the congeries of selves we all enclose
(Fascisti that we are,
bundles of stick-like selves, stick
figures awaiting ignition,
that when not transformed become
an emperor's mace) were activated —
but not so activated that they expanded into liberation
or abstraction, or a new conservatism.
Beckmann saw the tux coming in:
an "aristocratic" academy was to be pitted against Fascism.
In our time, rhymed verse associated with Pro Life,
        "free verse" associated with Fascism
by a middle class now filled with "artistic" hubris,
                which does not understand that
the artist is neither revolutionary nor conservative,
        but a worker of the between,
        a messenger from the centerless flux,
caretaker of the rational and the irrational. The divine is
stigmata and we are to express it. Think of us as a force being
torn apart by both the left and the right,

             the strength of Beckmann:
to record the multiple pulling for 40 years.

His mysteries bound in black leather radiate this inescapable paint.
Black becomes leading in the canvas-
cathedral shine of loosened invisibles.
He will not let go the desire to make burned
propellers gash through the auditorium of my morning.
"Everything is getting pretty funny and even more ghostly."
          fun   fuses   furor
       roars   with   horror
       *

The hour has come for the still-life:
                    flattened by Beckmann,
the figure refuses depth (grandeur).
The saxophone lies coiled around a Mexican pot,
          nearby a cactus is exuberating.
"Still-life" might include anything, for this room
in which "nature morte" is quietly panting
is a cage suspended in the abyss. About the scene,
"the great emptiness and uncertainty of space which I call God."
Inside the scene, the hunger of knowing no tasty
reward will be conveyed on the tray of a Hermic bellhop —
as a matter of fact, the bellhop hurries along past the cage.
A crown has been ordered by the executive in #408,
and because we are short on help these days
the messenger exercises a woman who pads along a cobalt sea.
"the sea, my old romance, it's been too long since I was with you.
You swirling eternity in your embroidered dress."

From the moment we first began to sense we ended,
from dawn at 14,000 BC when we found interiority at Niaux,
we have been dragging our shadows into
the functionless abattoir of the mind.
The mind contains a shadow-entrapment center,
yet the only results of the spiritual hunt are
the ghosts of animal hides over which
Beckmann's God's calcite is forming.

          20th century shadows break out like pox,
               striped measles,
welts sturdy as pieces of black fences he is hammering
against the God leaking dam, as if where he lives

is curse concrete to God's water.
"Iniquity lies in creation itself." "Unending divinity" indeed!

Creation. Catastrophe. The artist a demiurge turning
against the creator, a fish (or falling angel)
swerving against a bigger fish (or void)

The stumps, the bandages, the fetters

Blows against the body of God
*

The God splinters at log jam in his heart send out spikes of light,
gold-encrusted beams, swarming with harlequin ore.

He cauterizes ripeness with decay, individuals at intersection with
themselves.
Figures rush in, gods, non-gods, all screech to a halt, or screech to a
paint, as if we were caught in our hallway at night, at 10
fathoms, out of sleep for a drink, in the drink we found we were
still asleep, our entire body thirsty, the hallway bulging with all
the creatures of our imagination,
yet not solipsismal black, because I know that in my own dream
I am king, and a king committing suicide,
and that as I drive the dirk into my breast
it is the back of his muscular Columbine, whose back
I've never met, and as he appoints that back, he is involved
with telescopes, he can only reach himself as a shadowed
profile in a mirror. He sweats there, statue,
his big dumb feet sticking out below the sculptor's cloth,
and when he elbows his way out of the strait-jacket of baptism,
or twisted sheets, or thought-before-sleep,
he is heiling, with lopped-off-wrist, an Olympia busy as a rice paddy
in May.
His dream ends December 27, 1950, 10 AM, the corner of 61st Street
and Central Park West.

Why has no Western painter painted subincision?
The archangels of the *lower* body?
A woman really giving birth?
*

And he will not offer you a real foot, but the way your foot looks to
yourself,

211

which does not regard your foot in the same way as you do.
To you, foot is ideal foot, years ago heroic foot, now text book or
    media foot.
To your self, foot is the shape of your childhood foot,
something you grabbed for a thousand times in your crib, thus
your first sensation of pliable backbone,
the thing put in booties, a tennis shoe, Church shoe foot,
swimming pool fin foot, plaster casted,
invisible thus rotting, a foot with its own death, a chrysalis.
When you reveal your foot to your self, to the audience of your
    selves,
all the soul stances that have misidentified your foot,
what will your foot really look like?
    At 50, it is approaching your father. It gets whiter as you age,
    more — and less — marble.
The bones inside, victorious caterpillars.
This stump onto which you've stamped the invisible letter of your
    self.
The feet in Beckmann — that woman's calf — you've seen it at a glance
    from your car right
before turning onto the freeway, was it the way you mentally
    photographed her?
No, it was the accurate instant in which you saw her leg — her foot
    (you missed that),
what kind of dress was she wearing?
Why did her leg look like a wedge of paint?

We see out of embedded perceptions that snarl our selves
with honored images at home and at school.
What we totally look like is a perspective that belongs to the gods.
We have real feet, self feet, god hoofs.
What is pushed into my socks is an ending
freckled with innocence and filled with the guilt of stepping on snails.

Paradise is boudin-like   particle against particle

        *

"Nothing is left to us but protest — boundless contempt for the lascivious
bait with which we are repeatedly lured back to take life's bit in our mouths.
When we are half-dead of thirst, and want to quench it, the mocking
laughter of the gods appears."

His always-semi-nudes whose breasts like ice-cream cone scoops keep
    popping out of their bras,

212

so that the woman giving birth is ready for the next comer (the newborn is already elderly).
One can follow breasts in Beckmann like the bits of white bread left as a trail in the forest of so many tales,
or one can follow crowns, or drums, one can watch a road of things take on curbs, a seascape withdraw via the room and window we are viewing it through.
His impasto schizo candle flames, wet lemon tar, and the candle-sticks themselves, thugs, always asquirm with the otherwise questionable equilibrium, muffled waxen shouts that *more light* means *more dark.*
The soldier's dream is to be with his red-headed lass forever in a swimming pool, and he is, with a cage lowered over the pool, while the bugler who will wake both before they have embraced is already bugling, and the sleeping goddess he will never penetrate is holding up the clockface of departure—
Departure! The "unending divinity," the "great emptiness and uncertainty of space," is only center stage. At both sides, the obscenity off-stage is at full tilt. Ariadne and her two kings will never depart, for the heaven and hell wings of the triptych are inside us, bound to our pillars, bent over our crystal balls. The catch in the shallow hold of the archetypal skiff rots, but its putridness never turns to dust, for we all refurbish the loss with our own organs.

*

The manticores are singing with their triple bandsaw mouths.
They are singing the love song of Max Beckmann

"in that empty dining room . . . of the main train station in Frankfurt, beneath the pitiless white of the electric lighting, all alone with a bottle of champagne and a Brazilian cigar. There he sat, broad-shouldered, heavy, absent, thoughtful, observing the imaginary scene, no, the virtual reality, as keenly as if it had edges. There he leaned, pale, fixated in a cold fever, on his forehead beads of sweat like an exhausted porter who had thrown down his load . . . Never have I known such a lonely man. One could not seriously want to imitate him."

This corrosive song now blows through the LA County Museum, through the heads of the cistern folk assembled to wonder why art is so ugly. They had been wheeled in expecting a golden drop to fall from the tip of an archangel's sword into their wishing-well faces, but Beckmann was buffing his shoes in the corner, and when he looked up there was a fraying net filled with green, decomposing fish.

There were eyes in the side of the fish,
portholes giving vista to the submarine picnic
where the 400 pound nude rolled over into your salad and mine.
That's life, she explained, with trident and leash,
right here: the motionless whirlpool of the sink
yesterday's pasta, Perseus, and a blind organ-grinder
revolve in. And life is short at the wick,
while the flame itself extends in silken bands,

black fractures,
frilled poles,
cored orchids,
moral holes.

The beef of the abyss
shaking its bars.

Pelican tattooers
summoning Mars.

Acrobats roboting acts
on crutch-thrones,

crones
in the arms of winged
drones,

God on the band of a bicep
moaning
its steel chanson.

The OM spurting pike and
its OM flirting sister.

Lashed spine to spine:
the masquerade,
the turning marmelade,
the torpedo and
the blister.

Bucklered, caulked:
the vault in which
tuxedoed groom on
canvas bride are

forever displayed
before the gawkers,
the guards,
the burglars,
and the butts in the tray.

1985

THE EXCAVATION OF ARTAUD

Shaman of obsession—I said at his tomb—
excavated in electricity, opened between
anus and sex. In the Australian outback of the soul,
3 dead men are fingering your anesthetized root support
shining like a chain of sputtering lights, for the key to creation,
between the bone they've drawn out and your bone they so desire.

Priest of lethal phallic rites, of sparkings
in foetid material, of remaining in antithesis
with no hope of synthesis, priest of a genuine melee—
3 dead men are fingering your Muladhara Chakra, your amphimixis,
as if, under the Christian gunk that clogged your focus,
they could plug into your triangle and its twisting tongue of flame.

Pariah in silence, coprophilially
squatting in the corner of your cell for years,
sealed open, who only came when called by your mother's name—
repressing their way in, to the point of anal cancer,
3 dead men, licking your electroshock-induced Bardo, have found
your atomic glue, the Kundalini compost they must eat to speak.

O shaman, from having been so masterfully plundered!
O priest, from having been fixed in antithesis!
O pariah, from having been so desired by the dead!

1984

MAN AND BOTTLE

To be drunk is to be on knees praying
for the Queen of Flies to clamber up from her cellar,
step by step, through the beams and floorboards
and deliver to me the secret of death. That is my sole
desire here, as the wine passes through a second mouth
I've bored in my neck, and floods the rug out my left foot.
Will just a bit of it reach this Queen studying
her opened pus-colored book? I am sure at the end
of the wine's drooling meander there is a point at which
the Queen of Flies will be delighted, and smear
her vagina with this tincture as foreign to her
as my drunkenness is to me. Her book is sulphur yellow,
she opens it below the silty mineral light, and reads from it
on a table made out of bits of her lovers' husks. Sulphur
book on husk throne in the glow of minerals and her
excited crimson slit. The ointment sold by slugs does not
appeal to her, nor the rat hawking its scandal sheet to
a trolley packed with stoned cats. She reads the face of
Jesus in her book, she mutters, turning pus-page after
pus-page, she sees his desire appear as a mask
of yearning to be drunk on black wine, the wine of mites
and cockroaches, wine intense as steel, black-bladed wine
that separates fly head from fly abdomen and grafts in
the astonished Jesus face. This is the stunning frontispiece
in her Bible of Hell, and as she looks up at me in her violet
goggles, with a long fang of drool attaching her gums to
the page, I know that I get drunk to apply pressure to
that blushing savior, to force his head between
fly head and abdomen, as one turns a vise into itself,
to restore the integrity of a formlessness only recently
invaded by faith. More wine, I shout! Reeling and cork-
screwing down into the spider-swarmed rafters of
her transformational charts.

1985

SCARLET EXPERIMENT

The challenge of wholeness, to offer the lower
body imaginative status, so that the "negatives" of excrement,
menses, urine and semen, become intelligibles.
The tawny rocks panting like sponges, the whitened
violet dirt out of which asters are rocketing,
are as much a part of the Persian landscape in the vision of the
    Shah-nameh
as the prince, the maiden, and the necessary demon —
necessary because in this horned grotesca
the gods are more present than they are in us.

The apple dangling from the lovely fingers of a branch is red
all the way through, its seeds
tiny beings carousing in Eve's rich heart.
The earth, as well as woman, menstruates —
the evidence is flowers, especially roses.
Against green or brown, they take on a rusty,
delicious tenor, scarlet experiment
in league with liquid blackness, or that imperfect
circle of pebbles a male octopus arranges on the ocean floor,
to invite one in heat inside such a circle
to mate motionlessly changing colors for hours.

Forget the dragon. Think of George and maiden
lounged against an oak. He touches her vagina
and touches blood. The abyss moves forward, widens,
revealing a corridor in which red Ariadne is climbing forth,
8-legged menarche power returning from its winter sojourn with the
    nether Dionysus,
bleeding pinkly on its underworld path
which now unzips and rezips with the fervor of awakened dirt.

1984

An Epeira centered in her web, afloat yet anchored between ground and sky. The natural mind of the earth always spinning. Her one "decision," where to start the web. A small male enters, testing, sounding, the thread. At the center of the web, the penetrator is killed.

*

A Japanese Epeira, under whose green, red, and yellow abdomen I spider-sat, daily, for a month. One day, finding the web torn, I lamented a death, one that has never ceased to disturb me. The death of anything can contact the anythingness of our own death.

*

After Epeira disappeared, I had a vision during which, at the northwest corner of Nijo Castle, I saw a bright-red human-sized spider working a web up in the night air. The vision was too much for me. I did not have the language, the psychology, to report my own seeing of what I saw. Without Ariadne's thread, the veins, spittoons, claws, colorations and emanations of the goddess's body are opaque, not an image, a grueling picture.

*

At 85,000 BC, a foetally-tied corpse is carried on a pine-bough "raft" to a red ochre-packed pit in the German Neander Valley. Once deposited, the "corpse-raft" is covered with stone slabs. A few slabs have been discovered with cup-shaped indentations gouged in the side facing the corpse. The red-gated pit accepts the bound one—"then closes the Valves of her attention—like Stone." With the power of her red interior, she will wombify the entombed. A belief has persisted in primitive peoples that the soul, or the new-born itself, is a result of the coagulation of menstrual blood. In my spider vision, the green and yellow of Epeira's abdomen disappeared: the visionary spider was all red.

*

At 27,000 BC, 60 cup-shaped indentations were gouged in the form of a spiral in a large stone discovered at La Ferrassie. Red disks indicating vulva-like passage openings in the caves of Chufin and Pech-Merle, and the red vulva symbols in La Pasiega and El Castillo, indicate that at the very beginning of image-making, creation magic was related to menstruation. For the Arnhem Land Wawilak Sisters, the Rainbow Serpent is their synchronized menstrual power and its connections to coiling dragons, floodtides and storms.

*

The Wawilak Sisters' story has undergone a structural inversion and is now told in such a way as to help the men justify their having transferred women's mysteries into their own hands. They imitate menstruation and birth in artificial collective bleeding, gashing their arms and genitals, drawing subincisioned boys up between their legs. The women, humbled, go off into the bush to menstruate or give birth, alone. The men have torn apart the Sister web.

*

Let's erase the "Venus of" from the "Venus of Laussel." Let's restore Laussel, figurehead on the prow of the ship Earth, to her place-name identity. Originally colored red, she holds up a 13 notched bison horn, perhaps to link her desire with the animal's force as well as to synchronize her flow with his appearance. There is no bison body—only this horn which she tilts toward her turned head, a Scarlet Woman regarding the bison vortex.

*

Arachne is not Ariadne, although the figures are intertwined: the natural mind of the earth always spinning anticipates the mistress of the labyrinth that the initiate is to traverse. In the labyrinth of the creative life, "the bitter contest of the two natures" can be sublimated from a generational life/death struggle to an orgasmic union with a priestess whose lunar energies are at flood-tide.

*

Every artist everywhere participates in Ariadne. The transformation of the "given" life to a "creative" one not only involves entering a dark or "inner" life, but generating as well a resistance substantial enough to test oneself against and to shape the focus of one's work—and, having experienced the bestowal of soul (which is the reality of Ariadne), one must liberate the experience in a creative product, must emerge with more than the claim that something "happened" while "inside."

*

220

The earliest "pits" or earth-wombs were probably caves in which one to be initiated slept "in magical imitation of the incubatory sleep in the womb." We know that shamanic initiation involved long periods of incubation, pantomimed destruction, burial and rebirth. The incubus was not a perverse Christianized fiend, but an angel brooding on the initiate's body, perhaps in psychic imitation of the digger wasp/caterpillar conjunction. The signs, grotesques, and animals in Upper Paleolithic caves may have been painted there as dream allies, left as records of the dream/initiation, or both. The fact that this art is often found in remote and "tight" parts of a cave not only stresses the underground journey, but the crib-like congruence between the cave's body and the initiate's body.

*

The Minotaur of the early Cretan myth was named Asterior, synonymous with *aster*, "star." He was "bull and star at the same time," and the ultimate elevation of Dionysus and Ariadne, as a divine couple appearing in unmaimed, fully born, human form in the night sky suggests that the universe is the labyrinth and in imagination it is possible to be fully human there.

*

On the isle of Naxos, commemorating Ariadne's transformation, Theseus and his 14 companions danced a Le Tuc d'Audoubert-like swirling dance around a horned altar, which recalls actual bull horns through which Cretan bull-dancers flipped in a sacred marriage of the sun-king and the moon-goddess. The "horned altar" also evokes the womb's birth cone (and the labyrinth itself is prefigured by the cervix, lined with a branching called the "arbor vitae," or tree of life, where devouring white cells may be imagined to hide and wait like monsters for the Odyssean sperm over whose turbulent voyage the Athenic aspects of woman preside).

*

The horned altar is also the Double Axe, or labrys: bound together by a haft, the crescent-moon blades are a glyph of the labyrinth itself. Think of entering the lower tip of the left-hand crescent and following its curve to the haft, or center, where a change of materials signals an adaptation, through which one must penetrate, and readapt again in order to follow out the curve of the upper right hand crescent. The motion through is serpentine, and in respect to the material, the central confrontation is the movement from iron to wood to iron, organic vs. inorganic materials, which Wilhelm Reich layered to build his Orgone Accumulator, a small enclosure into which he invited patients, or initiates to his vision of a journey, on the peristaltic accordion of the body, from sexual insufficiency to orgastic potency.

*

As in Arnhem Land, where men took over women's menstrual mysteries and converted them into an attack on the body, there appears to be a take-over signified in the Cretan-Greek complex of myths relating to Ariadne. As Arihagne, the "utterly pure," a spinning hag or sorceress, she enjoyed intercourse with the labyrinth and its grotesque inhabitant. When patriarchal consciousness overwhelmed matriarchal centering, Ariadne became a "maiden to be rescued," who, "falling in love" with the hero Theseus, gave him the "clew" or thread that would enable him to get in and out and, while in, to slaughter the sleeping Minotaur. The labyrinth, without its central being, was thus emptied of animality.

*

In the 20th century, the burden of the vacated labyrinth involves hairline connections with the myriad cul-de-sacs of the deep past. The myth of Ariadne seems to capture much of Charles Olson's vision of "life turning on a SINGLE CENTER" until a mysterious "contrary will" manifested itself around 1200 BC, and the heroic attempt to "overthrow and dominate external reality" resulted in the migrational waves, or tentacles, that spread out around the planet. Do we in North America live in the bulb of a ten-tacle end that has, at the point it connects to a body, a slaughtered animal/hominid, whose corpse still fulgurates in our lethal dominational obsessions? Garcia Lorca's great and mysterious essay on the "duende" identifies this imp of the blood which provokes some of the world's great art as a struggle with a wound that never closes. Is Lorca therefore caught, whether he knows it or not, in Ariadne's turnstile, responding to a dark power of the blood that thousands of years ago mesmerized and enraged men as it appeared in rhythm with the moon and the tides and, without violence, ceased only to reappear again and again?

222

*

In Tantrik sexual magic, the two ingredients of the Great Rite can be *sukra* (semen) and *rakta* (menstrual blood). The sulphurous red ingredient in alchemical goldmaking may have been, in certain instances, this female essence (the *rubedo,* or precious red stone that sweats blood and turns the world to gold, is a conjunction of a whitened queen and a reddened King. Such a blending could be seen as a PINKENING). Many images of the labyrinth have not a minotaur but a rose at its center, a sign that a transformation has taken place. Seven days, across her period, the Old King is dissolved, rinsed of himself, his selves, lost in her "bath," her anabasis. The Dionysian initiate who is assimilated into this rose appears with a beard of roses to complement, below, Ariadne's rose-wreath crown.

*

The natural spinning mind of the earth weaves itself in personifications through our humanity. Biological peril is always central, the center, and sublimated by image-making into "scorpion hopscotch," or the imaginative gambling called poetry. It is possible to formulate a perspective that offers a life continuity, from lower life forms, through human biology and sexuality, to the earliest imagings of our situation, which now seems to be bio-tragically connected with our having separated ourselves out of the animal-hominid world in order to pursue that catastrophic miracle called consciousness. If the labyrinth is a Double Axe, one might see it as humanity's anguished attempt to center an unending doubleness that is conjured by the fact that each step "forward" seems to be, at the same moment, a step "backward." And the haft? Phallocentricity which fuses the menstrual/ovulatory cycles into an instrument of inner and outer ceremony that injures but does not restore.

1985

THE CRONE

I had tried to keep her balled up
in the bed sheets, not wanting to look at
the cancer, her terminal body, brown,
monkey-wizened, but she slipped out, unusually active,
her skin mahogany, more Indian
than I had thought my mother could be —
then I recalled the stories I had just heard about her,
how I was not my father's child, how I had
a brother, also not my father's — this news
excited me, and when she reappeared, capering
about the hospital room, she noticed I was erect
and laughed, Where did you get that? Oh I was joking
with some of my friends, I lied, still too innocent
to confront her black
ruby-rimmed eyes that twinkled in
flesh that had been used and used, as if I might
now put her on, a body glove. This is your true skin,
one voice said, and another: if you wear it
you will stave off the end of the world
for another cycle. I was so made of her by now
I had no place to go, and so began husking
to become her cob, her broomstick, her true husband.

1984

ARIADNE'S REUNION

I was called out into the forest to box
with a man I had been told represented
my other. I wore big blue gloves
and a nose mask; my other had only his hands,
and his unmasked face was more obscure
than any mask. We squared off in a clearing
and remained in that position forever,
for as soon as we recognized the extent to which
we mirrored one another, we both slipped out our backs,
he to quest with lantern for a younger man,
not that burlesque of virility I had put on.
As for me, I became a woman
lost in the image crowd pressing toward the arena,
that deep, tiered pit in the depths of which, lit
by flowing tapers, Ariadne, it was said, might appear
with her bull-headed partner. I took my place between two
who had jeered at Jesus as he struggled under
the immense onion onto which he was to be tied.
Gaunt jeerers, whose eyes brimmed with hail
as if the fools in the moon were emptying all their jugs.
Here, at the bottom of the world, one must move cautiously
between the thrust of narrative and
the associations the story sends out like feelers to test the air
for prey or rockface and if they do attach, a perpetual
give and take begins, for the older story wants to go on
and resists letting the new pull it apart as the new
revises the identity of the old. It is in the moment when
both have equal strength that Ariadne's face
is said to appear in this webbing —
at the moment the webbing tears, her bull-headed partner
bounds through. No one has actually
seen them couple — rather,
they have been memorialized as dancers,
thrusting in and out of gibbous circles
while the surrounding image crowd
receives the energy swarming out like tendrils unconcerned
with the crowd, tendrils that pass through
as if angling for something in the night sky
that would explode and cathect them on.

Look—she has appeared,
this evening in a spider mask to reveal why
no coupling, in living memory, has taken place.
In the blacker recesses of the pit,
to enter her is to be taken apart while one is inside.
The saying "no one has lifted her veil"
means that at the moment it is lifted
the lifter is no longer alive. Thus, her portal
is an active tomb, transforming the lifter into the goal
all desire: to carouse forever in her barque that floats above,
through white, red, and black weather, unphased
by the tiny spectacle below. Yet the story itself
seeks to destruct and to go on, and for this twist
both Dionysus and Theseus are required. One, it is said,
is her true husband, the other
a mistake. For ages it has been argued,
during intromission, why she gave Theseus
the clew to her animal heart. Theseus,
it is argued, had no intention of passing between
the horns, of losing himself in her arms to be
reclothed as a star. Theseus so resented her power
that he wanted to live forever in his own form,
and that is why he refused to tumble
and instead stabbed the sleeping Minotaur.
Why she allowed this to happen has never,
at least during intromission, been solved.
Some say her story follows natural evolution,
that one night her sacred victim recoiled
at the sight of her hideous threshold
or demanded to imitate, in his own way, her monthly flow.
Or that another host broke from the image crowd
and, with the victim, vied for her heart.
Leviathan and Behemoth, they churn in her gateway.
As the sun's hair is sheared, one fleshes out into a bull.
When the sun goes unpruned, the winning force is serpentine.
Then she is happiest, then she is most round.
But never as happy, many insist, as when pregnant by her true
    husband,
she gave birth before all assembled here.

            That was *the* night, one of my Jesus
jeerers whispered, that draws us back again and again to
Ariadne's Reunion. Frankly, to see her dance
with the bull-headed partner only makes us yearn more
for that night of nights. No one knew what was to happen,
yet as soon as she appeared, haggard, unmasked,

with a senile grin—and pregnant—we were all involved.
We sensed she had come so far that night,
much further than when she performed as a spider in the veiled
recesses of the pit. That night she was most used,
most virgin, and so entranced were we
that when, on her back, by herself, she pulled out
a glistening ear of corn, we fainted, for a moment
totally present, pregnant with the world in mind,
nourished into a vision that each thing
is a soul returned to mother
inspiration. It was then that cauldrons were brought forth,
and she beckoned all of us to enter. We sat,
naked, to our waists in warm fluid gently cooking
the tiny beings swimming around. They were dark red,
ringed, but peculiarly human. They nibbled
at our penises until, in alarm, we stood up
to discover we had no heads. Then we released
fans of blood-speckled milky substance and heard Ariadne call,
as if from the stars, NOW YOU MUST GET THE REST!
We reached up into our headless shafts
pulling out long knotted strings of octopuses and squids.
In joy we offered them to her, and as we did so,
we saw another dimension of what we were offering:
our own entrails, and that we were dead,
intensely alive and dead, and that one of her was squatting
over each of us, gazing madly into
the divinational cat's cradles she was making of our guts
as she bobbed up and down on our headless shafts.
O we were so happy to be anointed ones, christened
with her own oils so as to not injure her while she grooved!

1984

I BLENDED ROSE

The man who constellates Dionysus has entered
the arbor vitae where white cells cluster
to devour. He has stained his face cochineal
to blend—should he meet the Rainbow Serpent—
with its central stripe. He is the one
the Wawilak Sisters have chosen, the one they've summoned
to their water hole, to swim and to crawl while the water
over 7 days turns crimson. This man,
the water, and the Serpent, become one
force, the Sisters' thread or
twisty perception in the maze of otherwise
unintelligible nature. On the 3rd day
the man to become the vine is allowed
his first sip of cervix blood. On the 5th
he is slaughtered to imitate the flow. On the 7th
he kneels before the Sisters' horned altar
beholding the old moon in the new moon's arms.
For most men their own heart is the most
precious food. The man to become the wine
places his heart in the damp nest
of the Sisters' knotted towel. Faced with blood,
he mixes his sperm with the serpentine
bodies of the Sisters, he engages them at the haft
of the double labrys where
the waning and the waxing moons are hinged,
where energy reverses and the River of Life
becomes the River of Death. Dionysus is the force
that turns left to discover the Sisters' secret
child, the one who is to remain within,
neither totally animal nor totally human,
the one never to be delivered, who can only be accepted
as the reservation toward being, or who if not accepted,
must be killed. Dragged from the labyrinth,
this being is the Minotaur stabbed by the man
who refused transformation, who could only
imitate the Sisters' flow by gashing his own arms.
The man who constellates Dionysus discovers
at the central twist, instead of a beast,
an extraordinary rose, pink and blooming, illuminating

the recesses of meaning, the progeny of his white
and the Sisters' red. As they strum on his entrails,
he is blended, the harp of their reciprocal pit.

1984

DEEDS DONE AND SUFFERED BY LIGHT

One can glimpse Apollo in the door of each thing,
as if each thing now contains his oven —
in vision I open an olive tree and see his earlier animal
shapes fleeing at the speed of light, the python,
mouse, and lion Apollo, fleeing so that human forms
may walk unharmed by the invasion of the supernatural.
Light increased incredibly after the end of animal deity,
at the point verticality was instituted,
and the corpse of one's mother buried far, far from the place
on which one slept one's head. But the supernatural
in the guise of the natural is turning us over
in its fog a half mile from this ledge. Burnished
muscleless fist of a grey cloud. Sound of rain
from water still falling from the olives. I have no desire
to live in a world of nature conditioned by patriarchy.
I kick off my head and live in the light
bounding in from my mother. It is her great
ambivalence toward her own navel that conditions
the decreasing dripping. The hills now
writhe with green meat and something should follow.
Something should be explaining the tuft of salmon bull shape
abandoned by the other stilled clouds. Something
should be done with the swatted fly. Something is
this abyss of unusableness that remainders me
and pays no royalty. There are hosts of thrones
directly above. A witch hammer. A cleated enclosure.
The way a church has of making you puke your soul
upon entering and then, as the dryness of birth is rehashed
by nun and candle, of worshipping what has just left you,
the bride of your chest, the stuff inside you that a moment before
twinkled with the sadness and poverty of the street's
malicious laughter. How I wish that this poem
would birth another, and that the other had something to do
with unpacking the olive meat of this mountain. No
apocalypse. An enlargement, rather, of the so-called Whore
on her severely underfed Dragon. And more wine. More plumes
of silver azure evening coursing over
the thatch of the mountainside. More space to suffer,
more farewell to the flesh, more carnival in the face of everyman,
less perfection, more coherence. Meaning: more imagination,
more wigs for glowworms, more cribs for the restless dead

who wake us right before dawn with their bell leper
reminding us that fresh rain air is a clear indication
that here is not entirely here. The processions of graffiti-
scarred bison are, like us, clouds imprisoned to be viewed.
And then my mother began to speak: "You've put on a lot of
    weight!
Look at your father and me, some shape we're in! We've suffered
a lot for you these 14 years. You should've seen my left side
when it turned into a purple sponge and stained what
you buried me in to the point it rotted. I'm glad
John Ashbery appeared to you last night reading new
incomprehensible poems that made perfectly good sense. You are
much more organized, much more chaotic, than you behave here.
When I think of you, I see you at 12, stuck in the laundry chute,
your legs wiggling in the basement air, while the top part talked
with me as we waited for the renter to pull you out.
We had a nice chat that afternoon, and I almost liked you best
that way, just what stuck out of the chute. If I could only have
that part on a roller skate and let what was wiggling below go—
it's that part that's gone off gallivanting,
that's carried you goodness knows where while I
and your father lie here a few feet away from each other
waiting for our coffin lids to cave in. Then, even
the little space you left us to play with memories of you
on our chest bones will be gone. My buttons are mouldy
and my hands have no flesh left but I still manage
to squeak my buttons a little and get into your dreams.
I'm sorry if I appear both dead and alive to you,
but you should know by now you can't have it your way all the
    time.
I'm as real in this way as I ever was, sick more often than not
when I appear, but you're never here, you're worrying
how to take care of me, and then you wake to a jolt
every time there's nothing to take care of.
Now your father wants to say a word." "Clayton,
why don't you come home? We were such a nice little family.
Now it is like when you went off to that university.
Your mother and I would sit up and talk about you
until our fathers came in from the night and motioned us
into our bed. You were such a nice little fellow
when we could hold you up high and look at each other
through you. Ten little fingers ten little toes
Two bright eyes a funny little nose
A little bunch of sweetness that's mighty like a rose
Your mother, through you, looked so much like
your grandmother I could never get over it.

Why I bet you don't even remember your birth gifts
a savings bank and one dollar from granddad and grandmother
Two kimonas from aunt Georgia and uncle Bob
Supporters from Faye's dollie Patricia Ann
A Romper Suit from Mrs. Warren Bigler
A Dress from Mr. & Mrs. SR Shambaugh
Silk Booties & Anklets Knit Soaker & Safety Pins
Hug-me-tight a Floating Soap Dish with Soap Rubber Doggie
I don't see why you don't come home. Your mother and I
have everything you need here. Why sure,
let's see, maybe you could pick up some things,
Gladys — no, she's not listening — *Gladys what do you want?*"
"Well, I know we need some scouring powder and light bulbs"
"GLADYS WHAT DO YOU WANT?" "And Clayton, we want
Clayton to come back we don't like Clayton Jr. out so late at night"
"GLADYS WHAT DO YOU WANT?" "You never know what will
    happen, why
just last week Eunice Wilson, over in Plot #52541, told me"
"GLADYS WHAT DO YOU WANT?" " — are you listening, Daddy?
Eunice said while Jack was getting out of his car parked in his own
    driveway at 2 AM"
"GRADDISROTDUYRUNT!" " — after his date with Kay Fisbeck,
    this man
came up to him and said something I will not"
"GRADDISROTDRURUNT" " — I will not repeat it was that
    vulgar —
this man said: if you don't come with me, I'll crush your cows.
Doesn't that take the cake? Why Clayton you can't blame Jack
for going off with him, and you would not believe where
this man took Jack Wilson and what he wanted him to do.
Now that your father's lid has caved in, I'll tell you:
he made him drive north to the Deaf School parking lot,
and when he was sure nobody else was around, he said:
        Persephone's a doll
            steeper than Marilyn,
        miracles lick her,
            dreams invader,
        over the cobweb orchestra
            there's an ice
            conductor,
        forget the orchestra,
            conduct the pit!
        Hanged
        Ariadne
            giving birth in Hades
        is the rich, black music in mother's tit."

THE MAN WITH A BEARD OF ROSES

A constructed indwelling, an antiphonal swing.
These were the things that mattered
to the man for whom the goddess wreath
was truer to the earth he knew than a barbwired heart.

Because he had loved and been loved by
the person he most desired to be with and to talk to
he could die at any time. He would not
have missed the central frosty drop

every mother's cuddling proclaims will fall.
But he did not desire nonbeing. He desired to throw
back the curtains of every day and enter
the cave of flowers where mature transformations

intermingled with the immature. He desired,
therefore, he depended. No matter that his appetite
was infantile, that he never really rested,
that his beard was also barbed. He knew he would never

assimilate his points. That he had many,
not merely one, was a multitude and kept him aloft
on a road whose wavy grain he went against
as he journeyed through it, or simply went

with a sideward wash to find once again he'd been
deadended, or had he descended — or blended?
Words were walls worth boring through, worth
turning into combs, words were livable

hives whose centers, or voids,
sounded the honey of emptiness dense
with the greyish yellow light nature becomes
to the soul for whom every thing is a cave

or hollow in the top of a water demon's
head, a green being plunging into green, sound
eating color, a sentence rolling closure
away from its opening. Inside this man the brutal

world had died. He felt its rot in every pore,
its disappearance in the sinew of his petals.
He had lived its life, but even more his own,
against the bio-underpinning to simply flex like worms.

1984

DEDICATION

There is a part of me that still feels that the poet himself is solely responsible for what he writes. And since I have never accepted the high Romantic ideal that I was a radio set, or a secretary, filtering the messages, garbled or in code, from another "place," I have come to believe that the only way poetry can be restored as an active agent in everyone's life is for the poet to be the responsible one as well as the inspired one, to maintain the unity of reason and sensation.

Blake's authors in eternity are also secretaries, for the origin of archetypal address, if there is one, is closer to 30,000 BC than to early Greek Gods. While there is, thus, no pure or true message, twentieth-century art has continued to be inhabited by a divisive and old-fashioned sense of the artist as divine child or idiot, daft under full moon, the magical receiver, thus in need of the rational framing of a critic or psychologist to explain him, since from such a perspective the artist is irresponsible. The trick is to make him feel that he is privy to sensations and messages that evade the "common person"—and then make him pay through the mind for this "privilege." I believe that I am responsible for every word that I write, and if I am beside myself at times, if the words appear to come from elsewhere, this is a gift that I must honor but also evaluate as it appears before me in the process of composition.

At the same time, I thank Caryl here, in this dedication, not as the traditional "acknowledgement," but for her active participation in the writing in this book since the early 70s, when I began to show her what I was doing and to ask her opinions about whether it made imaginative sense or not. I only publish around 10% of what I write, and as far as I am concerned, the muse/angel/duende complex can be present or not at any stage of this process—the process of transforming, say, 100 pages of writing into 10 pages that read "right," as poetry to be shared with others.

To dedicate this book to Caryl is mainly to thank her for her role between the 100 and the 10 pages, for going over page after page with me, at the table together, in the morning after coffee, and asking me thousands of questions about what I meant by this or that, why did I write this or that, in other words, for helping me to narrow down the infernal discrepancy between what I thought I had written and what I did write, or how it would appear to an intelligent, literate person without any particular cult or movement ax to grind.

I want to emphasize that I am not thanking Caryl for approving of my writing, or for "following" me in my various literary activities. To do so would miss the point of this dedication. For while I am responsible for initiating and completing these poems, Caryl has been a major force in the middle passages, often rewriting or reconstructing a mass of material that I knew had real worth but did not know how to successfully complete by myself.

In the beginning, I was unsure as to whether I should share this activity with anyone. Being unsure meant that to share it with Caryl was a constant assault on my ego, offering my convictions on this or that to a test that often came down to whether what I had written made any kind of imaginative or even common sense. I think that this activity has been, and continues to be, one of the best things that has happened to me as a poet.

What I am attempting to describe is a kind of groundwork in which all the new materials, the risks, the leaps, the dreams, are to be shared and considered in tandem with another while they are in process, often with no plan or solution at hand. To do this considerably extends the compositional period, and creates a situation which seems to have many more branch-offs than what I would allow myself as a writer by myself. Caryl has often picked up seed ideas or near images in a worksheet that when urged forth in dialogue have made me realize that another range of materials has been stimulated, and that for me to be responsible for the new potential of a particular passage, I must do more homework on what I before had hoped to touch on and pass beyond.

I want to say more about the assault on the ego that working together involves. To practice any art seriously in North America today means that one must have a very strong sense of oneself as doing something meaningful in a context that for the most part, and perhaps for the most significant art in the long run, has no audience at all. One works in a vacuum, as a kind of hip autistic figure plugging oneself into whatever gods or energy deposits are available, at the same time that one is haunted by the feeling that one is more in contact with nature and literature than with most people. To what extent this situation is true is impossible to determine. I mention it because the artistic conviction necessary to mobilize a body of work is its own obstruction.

One must amass so much energy and directive to make what one does hold, in vacuum, that it is impossible to transform all of it into the created product. What is not transformed tends to become ego fortification, thus proposing that the poem is great because it was written by a great poet — not the other way around, that the poet is great because he has written great poems. One ends up protecting his holdings while creating his holdings, in short-circuit to his own process, a schizophrenia within the binary inner and outer world transmission every artist must learn to regulate.

A central outcome of this for post-WW II poetry is the weakening of the fictional or imaginative ego which handles the bridge-work between the past descriptive ego and those terrified aspects of the self that want to jettison all focus on one's personal experience. In between these two poles, neither of which is capable of expressing how it is to live in 1985, are the Vallejos, Artauds, Celans, and Holans who live in the conflict of all extremes, with a sense of personal voiced integrity that is not at the mercy of merely recounting or intentionally obscuring its unrealized experience.

I look back in this book at the poems in the 60s whose autobiographical "I" was even uncertain, where a confidence to speak for myself, to stand by my own

238

word, *often seemed impossible to achieve. By the early 70s, I felt that the personal voice had been sufficiently created to enable it to split into either fictional voicings (mainly the "Portraits") or a perspective generated by the poem under hand, in which a non-identifiable "I" roamed the poem, shaped and restricted by the poem's own meanderings.*

Since the 70s, I have believed that Caryl's participation was not only encouraging a more coherent poetry but a focus that increasingly had criticized the singleness of my background. Because of her, I have come to believe that "I" is the most open word in the language, that poetry is still in its psychological infancy, and that rather than repressing such troubling and unstable forces as "the self" or "the ego," that they should be opened up and explored. Because our national self has become monstrous, it is not easy to do this, and the tendency of too much poetry, in my opinion, has been to either treat the "I" as a tried and true beacon by which one can beam one's experiences at the world, or to negate it entirely (forcing the entire poem, as it were, to bear its diffused weight). I believe that to actively imagine one's own experience within the negations of capitalistic or communistic society is now a perilous but necessary task.

Thank you for these days, Caryl, and the late afternoons, and the evenings, thank you for providing a readership of the heart, a hearing that complexly sent forth its flotillas of response, the immediate response of one who is also the beloved. Had you not been here I would have lost, ruined, torn apart possible poems because as an only child the hardest thing I have had to learn to believe in has been not just the apparition of the other, but her friendship, the ways in which "muse" can be present in the dialogue of two people. Who said inspiration takes place alone?

1985

NOTES

The notes that follow are far from complete. They form a compromise between my hesitancy to offer any at all (believing that they are ultimately part of the scholar's responsibilities) and my desire to say something about everything that might block the reader. I have not annotated acquaintances, defined figures that can be found in mythological encyclopedias, or (with a few exceptions) referred the reader to published poems not included in *The Name Encanyoned River* that reinforce or amplify poems here. What I have tried to do is to note most of the esoteric sources, and to indicate some of the concerns in the constellation of the reading I have done and fed into the poems since the early 60s.

CE / March, 1985

I / THE COASTAL OVENS
(1960-1970)

The Book of Yorunomado

Tú, luego, has nacido: from César Vallejo's poem, "El Alma Que Sufrió De Ser Su Cuerpo." "NO. LA MANO, HE DICHO" is from the end of the same Vallejo poem.

Tsuruginomiya: "Sword Shrine," a Shinto temple complex facing the Ibuki home in Kyoto where Barbara Eshleman and I rented quarters in 1963-1964.

The Darkening of the Light: see Hexagram 36, Wilhelm/Baynes tr. of the *I Ching*. The quoted material in a subsequent poem, "The Yellow Garment," concerning K'un (Hexagram 2), is from The Commentaries on the *I Ching*, Part I.

THE DUENDE: according to Garcia Lorca (in "Theory and Function of the *Duende*"), "we must repel the angel, and kick out the muse; the real struggle is with the *duende,* which burns the blood like powdered glass and rejects all the sweet geometry one has learned." This section of the poem is also pervaded with material from the 1962 Japanese film, *Seppuku* (= harakiri = ritual disembowelment).

Niemonjima II

Niemonjima is a Japanese island (visited by Basho on one of his extended hikes), off Yokohama. Like the Yorunomado coffee-shop, it takes on symbolic import

241

that has nothing to do with Japanese mythology, but which is related to Enithar-
mon and Los, Blake's figures for Spiritual Beauty and Poetry. The attempt,
as in Blake, is to restrict the figure's reference to the poems' contexts; think
of them as home-made archetypes.

Sepik Delta: my phrase based on Sepik River culture of New Guinea, and the
Phi Delta Theta social fraternity at Indiana University where I lived, 1953-1956.
"The double fireplace" was a huge two-way hearth at the center of the Phi
Delt livingroom when the fraternity was at the corner of 10th Street and Jor-
dan, in Bloomington, Indiana, in 1953.

O holy Generation: see Blake's *Jerusalem,* Pl. 7. "Whenever any Individual . . ."
is from his "A Vision of the Last Judgment." "Origin's watchfiends" is a turn
on Blake's "Satan's Watchfiends," against the view of poetry proposed by *Origin*
magazine and editor Cid Corman. The phrase, "the moment of desire,"
originates in Blake's *Visions of the Daughters of Albion.* In a subsequent poem,
"the 1802 Blake Butts Letter Variation," Jesus's speech to Albion appears on
Pl. 96 of *Jerusalem.*

Ode to Reich

clarification of Beulah: a fusion of Reich's theory of the function of the orgasm
with Blake's interpretation of "Beulah," i.e., the world of gratified desire leading
to imaginative vision and work (a sighting of Maithuna and the "antiphonal
swing" elaborated throughout these poems). For a discussion of the differences
between Freudian and Blakean sublimation, see Harold Bloom's *The Visionary
Company,* pp. 16-29.

II / SCORPION HOPSCOTCH
(1972-1979)

Creation

the Venus of Lespuge: Upper Paleolithic "Great Goddess" statuette from
southwestern France, dated around 22,000 BC. The last two stanzas of the
poem draw on material in Marcel Griaule's *Conversations with Ogotemmêli.* A
subsequent poem, "Magdalenian," is based on another "Goddess" statuette from
the Late Magdalenian period (roughly 11,000 to 8,000 BC), which appears to
never have had a head.

Ira

a natal daemon: the phrase comes from Porphyry's "Concerning the Cave of the
Nymphs," including translator Thomas Taylor's footnote on Ulysses' adven-
ture with the Cyclops. The figure is elaborated in a subsequent poem, "The

Natal Daemon," in which the quote is also from Porphyry's Neoplatonic treatise.

Scorpion Hopscotch

as Berdyaev and Bataille have said: for Nicolas Berdyaev, see the chapter on Creativity and Sex in *The Meaning of the Creative Act*; for Georges Bataille, see both *Eroticism* (also translated as *Death and Sexuality*) and the *Lascaux* monograph.

Still-life, with African Violets

Yunotsu: a mineral spa in southwestern Honshu, Japan, where Barbara Eshleman and I, by chance, bathed with scarred atomic bomb survivors in 1964.

The Name Encanyoned River

"For the past 6 years, José Rubia Barcia and I have been retranslating my earlier translation of César Vallejo's "Poemas Humanos," and we have used the 1968 Moncloa edition of Vallejo's Obra Poética Completa to check our work against because it reproduces a good deal of the poet's original corrected typescript. As Barcia and I neared the end of the retranslation, I was struck by a line in the poem called "Piensen los Viejos Asnos" that Vallejo himself had crossed out: at the end of the 19th line he originally wrote: "le llamaré del margen de su nombre de río encajonado!" It seemed to me one of those lines that are beautiful in themselves but which get eliminated because they do not work in the context they were written into. At this time, I knew that I was on the verge of a big poem in which the weight of the 16 years spent with Vallejo was to be expressed, balanced and resolved — and that line flew out at me as a place to dig in."

CE / 1977

II / THE SEPARATION CONTINUUM
(1978-1982)

Placements I

Le Portel: Le Portel, and the subsequently mentioned Les Trois Frères, Gargas, Lascaux, Le Tuc d'Audoubert, Abri Cellier, and Niaux, are all caves or rock shelters in southwestern France, decorated by Cro-Magnon (= big hole) people, roughly between 25,000 and 10,000 BC, during the last phase of the Upper Paleolithic period, in which humankind made the transition from no image to an image of the world, and created the first art that we are aware of. For more material on what I call "Paleolithic Imagination and the Construction of the Underworld," see *Hades in Manganese* (1981), and *Fracture* (1983).

the other side of nature: see Rilke's "An Experience," in *Selected Works,* Vol. I, Prose. Tusex stores are government-operated "luxury" marts which require the use of special money easily obtained by foreigners but difficult for those behind the Iron Curtain to come by.

Un Poco Loco

"Un Poco Loco" is a bebop composition by Bud Powell; three "takes" can be heard on Blue Note LP #1503.

The Aurignacians Have the Floor

The Aurignacians were the first Cro-Magnon people to make figurative art (deeply incised animals, human sexual and abstract signs in limestone slabs) starting around 32,000 BC. Thus they *are* the floor, and they should be "given the floor," rather than being dismissed with a brief mention, at best, in "history of art" books. A companion poem, "The Aurignacian Summation," is in *Fracture.*

Notes on a Visit to Le Tuc d'Audoubert

"tanist" re. Graves: see the Introduction of Robert Graves' *The Greek Myths.* "Tanist" is an ancient Irish word for the sacred king's "twin," or "lieutenant," who would succeed his rule. Mikhail Bakhtin's *Rabelais and His World* is an important source for ideas concerning "grotesque realism" in the last three sections of this book. See also the Introduction to *Fracture* for a discussion of the "grotesque archetype." For a photo of the two clay bison (and an illuminating discussion of Upper Paleolithic art in general) see S. Giedion's *The Eternal Present,* pp. 394-395.

Coproatavism

This narrative draws on material from the "bison chamber" at Le Tuc d'Audoubert, and the contemporary case of a disturbed adolescent who placed his turds around his sleeping room-mate and then danced around him (I have substituted my own "Ira" for the room-mate's name in order to get at another aspect of the natal daemon). For copious examples of the ancient and worldwide phenomena of the ritual use of excrement and urine, see John G. Bourke's *Scatologic Rites of All Nations.*

Visions of the Fathers of Lascaux

Most approaches to the meaning of Upper Paleolithic art stress survival concerns and involve various rehashings of "the hunting hypothesis." Here I have sought to explore a vision that behind and within cave wall art is a crisis that went on for some 20,000 years: the separation of the hominid/animal constitution (thus "the separation continuum," the title of this section of the book). See also the extended note on this poem in *Fracture*.

Maithuna.

"It is in this afterglow after sex that the things of God are revealed; the tantrics call it Maithuna." *The Wise Wound,* by Peter Redgrove and Penelope Shuttle.

II / ANTIPHONAL SWING
(1983-1985)

Tuxedoed Groom on Canvas Bride

All the quotes, save one, are by Beckmann himself, and can be found in Carla Schulz-Hoffmann's essay, "Bars, Fetters, and Masks," in *Max Beckmann — Retrospective* (The St. Louis Art Museum, 1985). Wilhelm Hausenstein's description of Beckmann in the train station restaurant is quoted in the biographical section of the same catalog.

The Excavation of Artaud

This poem is based on a prosodic pattern by Vallejo in the poem "El libro de la naturaleza." Artaud mentions the attack on his Muladhara Chakra (= root support), or, in his own words, "that bone / located between anus and sex," in *Artaud the Mômo* (for which see *Antonin Artaud: Four Texts*). In *The Masks of God: Primitive Mythology,* Joseph Campbell quotes Geza Róheim on Australian black magic directed against "the flesh between the scrotum and the rectum." The term "amphimixis" (= the synthesis of two or more erotisms in a higher unity) was coined by Sandor Ferenczi in *Thalassa.*

Placements II

Sources for this reading of Ariadne include: *Dionysus* by Karl Kerényi; "The Gate & the Center" by Charles Olson (*Origin* #1, Spring 1951); *The Gate of Horn* by G. R. Levy; "Levi-Strauss and the Dragon" by Chris Knight (*Man,* #18, March 1983); *Le Mystère des Cathédrales* by Fulcanelli; *The Thread of Ariadne* by Charles F. Herberger; *The Wise Wound* by Peter Redgrove and Penelope Shuttle; *The Woman's Encyclopedia of Myths and Secrets,* edited by Barbara G. Walker; exchanges with James Hillman; the modal legacy of the Cro-Magnon people.

Printed January 1986 in Santa Barbara & Ann
Arbor for the Black Sparrow Press by Graham
Mackintosh & Edwards Brothers Inc. Design
by Barbara Martin. This edition is published
in paper wrappers; there are 300 hardcover
trade copies; 150 copies have been numbered
& signed by the author; & 26 lettered copies
have been handbound in boards by Earle Gray
each with a holograph poem/drawing
by Clayton Eshleman.

CLAYTON ESHLEMAN was born June 1, 1935, in Indianapolis, Indiana. He was educated at Indiana University and has traveled widely, living in Japan, Korea, Peru, and France. In 1979 he shared the National Book Award, with José Rubia Barcia, for *César Vallejo: The Complete Posthumous Poetry.* He has been the recipient of a Guggenheim Fellowship in Poetry, a National Endowment for the Arts Poetry Fellowship, a National Endowment for the Humanities Translation Fellowship to translate Aimé Césaire, and a National Endowment for the Humanities "Summer Stipend" to support his ongoing research on "Paleolithic imagination and the construction of the underworld." From 1979 to 1984, he was the Dreyfuss Poet in Residence and Lecturer in Creative Writing at the California Institute of Technology, where he founded *Sulfur* magazine in 1980.